# Ink-Filled Page

# Ink-Filled Page

*Red Anthology*

Indigo Editing & Publications

**Indigo Editing & Publications**
P.O. Box 1355
Beaverton, OR 97075
*info@indigoediting.com*
*www.indigoediting.com*

**Copyright © 2009** by Indigo Editing & Publications

*Ink-Filled Page, Volume 3*

Senior Editor: Ali McCart
Production Editors: Kim Greenberg, Kori Hirano, Hannah Kingrey,
Megan Wellman
Proofreaders: Kelsey Connell, Lisa McMahan
Cover and Interior Design: Wise Design

ISBN: 978-0-9819422-1-6

Printed in the United States of America

*Ink-Filled Page* is published quarterly online at *www.inkfilledpage.com*
and compiled into a print anthology annually by Indigo Editing &
Publications. Subscribe at *www.inkfilledpage.com*.

**Submission deadlines are:**
Spring Youth Issue (grades 6–12): February 28
Summer Issue: May 31
Autumn Issue: August 31
Winter Issue: November 30

**Submit fiction, nonfiction, and artwork at:**
*www.inkfilledpage.com/submissions*

# Table of Contents

# Artwork

# Introduction

Life is not primary colors. We don't see our families and landscapes in crayon red, blue, and yellow with bold black outlines. Instead, we are blessed with brilliant, contrasting shades—strawberry, salmon, carnation, brick, and deep blood. The canvases of life are swept with broad strokes and intricate detail, subjects ranging from yearnings for what we cannot have to rejecting what will not leave.

And so art reflects life. As we read, we journey into the creators' worlds, unable to keep ourselves from dipping our own brushes into the various hues laid before us. We are sideswiped in a rush of harsh green when our bodies betray us, but cobalt brings us home, sometimes only to peer in the windows before moving on. Lemon fills the sky when we look back on a land that was once ours, but faded sienna stains the life we never meant to have. And there's always red—those people in our lives, both loved and hated, whom we pull closer in a scarlet embrace and then shove to crimson exile.

And after all that, we fade to white. To the empty page, waiting to be filled again.

—Ali McCart

# Nonfiction

# Child of Mine
*Marian Burke*

I study the silver speckles in the blue linoleum
floor, searching for a pattern, some sort of order in
the chaos. My forehead is pressed against the edge
of the mattress as I sit, bent over, in a hard chair
beside her hospital bed. My daughter's hand rests
on the back of my neck where my hair is damp and
curling from the rain that fell in sheets as I stood
panicked and dumb outside the ambulance. I lift
my forehead off the edge of the bed and look at her
ashen face, so perfect in its paleness.

"I'm sorry," she whispers, tears welling up,
chocolate swirls above the white of her cheekbones.
Charcoal spittle clings to the corners of her mouth,
and her teeth are tinged with gray as if she has
just finished a licorice Slurpee. I wonder where my
antidote is. Sighing, I reach for her hand, close mine
around it, and marvel at the smallness of it. How
can it still be so small? I clear my throat to ward off
my own threatening tears. Her other hand, connected by plastic tubing to an IV bottle suspended above
her bed, reaches out to touch my face, and I snap my

head up and away, out of her reach. I do not let go of the little hand I am holding, though—I clutch it as tightly as I used to when she was five years old and about to step off the sidewalk into the street.

"I just wanted it to stop," she says. Simple, no elaboration, just so.

I lower my head back to the bed and digest this.

I want it to stop too. I realize that for the first time in a very long time, we are on common ground. She pulls her slender hand away from mine and curls it under her chin. She is tired, she says. I am tired too (another thing to share), and my weariness pounds behind my eyelids like a heartbeat.

The doctor comes in, and I sit straighter, trying to focus on the words he is saying. Is he speaking to me or to her? She is answering him, a little girl's voice chirping through black-rimmed lips.

"I don't know how many I took, maybe twenty or twenty-five," she says. "I was looking for Tylenol—I had a headache, I guess. Then I saw the other pills, and…I didn't plan it, or anything. I was just standing there with a headache and just so tired of it all, and it came to me—it seemed like the only way. I just wanted to make it stop," she repeats her plaintive refrain.

I try to listen to the doctor explaining how she was lucky she did not take twenty to twenty-five Tylenol while I envision my child standing in front of our medicine chest, reaching out for a bottle of muscle relaxants. Her liver would be mush, he says. I find that odd. Mush. Is that what doctors say? He places his hand on my shoulder as he leaves. Hang in there, it seems to say, fingers squeezing.

We are alone again, and she asks for something to eat. I look into her dark eyes, hungry to see her in them. She is not there.

Food. I am eager to see her eat. I want to watch her mouth open and close, see her throat work the morsels down into her belly. I want to feed her myself, holding the spoon in front of her, my own mouth open to show her how. My chest constricts with guilt. I should have breastfed her.

I raise myself up from the chair, and I feel heavy. It is hard work just to stand there. I walk out of the room, past the policeman who sits in a wooden chair just outside the door, past the woman writhing on a gurney in the hall, her hospital gown hitched up, exposing thigh and dimpled buttock. I avert my eyes from hers—she is too much in them. I cannot afford to see her.

The man in the next room is vomiting and yelling obscenities between retches. The nurses ignore him, but I cannot. He is mad. But in his madness, I see beauty, a freedom that beckons me. I could scream and retch and let my ass hang out of my johnny and just let go. I turn from the puking man, stopping up my ears with the palms of my hands to drown out his siren's call.

The nurse tells me the cafeteria is on the third floor. Go right at the end of the hall, take the west elevators up to three; go past the gift shop, to the left. In the elevator, two medical students discuss a patient while I read the hospital's privacy statement on the wall. I try not to listen, thinking how ashamed I would be if I were the subject of their discussion. I begin to cry. I weep as if I am alone. Like a child, I heave great gulping sobs that cannot be stifled even though my fist is stuffed into my mouth. The medical students stop talking and look at each other for direction. They are all facts and techniques with no real sense of what is needed to truly heal someone.

The elevator doors open, and I rush out, turning to look at the young man who enters after me. He is carrying a bouquet of roses and a stuffed pink bear with a bib proclaiming *It's a Girl!* in festive lettering.

The young man's chin is dark with stubble, and he looks happy as he pushes the button for his floor. He has no clue.

The hallway leading away from the elevator is lined with artwork. I notice one abstract painting that reminds me of her because she would get it. Where I see only kindergarten splats of color, she would see conflict, wisdom, resolution.

My sobs subside as I think about the painting of a lighthouse that she did in oil. It hangs in my bedroom, and I love the detail of the waves as they crash against the rocks in the foreground. I am always amazed at how she was able to capture the colors of the sea so perfectly—deep green, midnight blue, Caribbean turquoise, pure white. She hates the painting, a classroom project she was forced to complete. She detests any art that is representative, preferring to cull her own meaning from less accessible works.

The cafeteria is deserted. Only the vending machines offer any hope. I agonize over my choices, wanting to fill her up with wholesome goodness. I contemplate running home to stuff and roast a chicken, then laugh out loud at the idea. My laughter echoes in the empty cafeteria and it sounds edgy and lunatic. I watch my dollar bill slip in and out of the vending machine like a mocking tongue.

I return to the elevator empty handed, a failure. I push the button for the fourth floor. She is in the basement, but I am going up. The elevator carries me higher.

The doors open to another hallway adorned with Anne Geddes photographs. Pudgy new faces peek out of daisies, peonies, and lion's manes. Naked babies rest snug in walnut shells and peapods, as if that is how they got here.

I should not be here, yet I turn down the corridor and walk until I come to the observation window. I watch them, all lined up in rows, wrapped tight in straitjacket swaddling, their little faces not really like those in the pictures. Some of these new faces are red or pinched and swollen. Some have tiny starbursts of broken capillaries on the puffs of their little cheeks. It isn't easy, I think, even now.

I stand in front of the window long enough to see the man from the elevator enter the room with a young woman in a pale yellow chenille robe with matching slippers. She looks tired, the color of the robe emphasizing the pallor of her skin and the dark bruise-like circles under her blue eyes. It never changes—it is just one long exhaustive labor.

I return to the elevator and descend the four flights to the emergency room. Retracing my steps, I stop to look in on the beautiful madman next door. He has been replaced by an elderly woman. She reclines, stiff in the bed, her mouth frozen open in a toothless gape through which she sucks in rasps of dry air. Her eyes scream curses at the obscenity her life has become. I look away, aware of her watching me do so.

I nod to the policeman as I pass. He smiles back, a kind smile that says he has been here a dozen times before and he can assure that this one is going to be just fine. She isn't like the others he's seen—she

isn't really crazy; she doesn't have parents who are as bad off as she is. His simple, reassuring smile and assumption that I am a good mother threatens to overwhelm me, and I swallow a sob before it can escape.

Next door to the old woman, a young woman, my daughter, lies sleeping. Her mouth is open, and she is breathing through it noisily. Her face has pinked up a bit beneath its cap of unnatural auburn hair. I notice an empty apple juice container and two half-eaten cups of gelatin, green and orange, her least favorites.

I lower myself back into the wooden chair and rest my cheek against the cool of the metal rail someone has raised in my absence. She is safe here, taken care of; her needs are being met. I look at my watch.

"Why don't you just leave?" she says. Her eyes look right into mine, and I can see that she feels she has just caught me at something. I reach out and brush a wisp of hair away from her eyes. I lower the rail and rest my forehead once more on the bed. I cannot speak to her.

"I'm glad I called you," she says, her tone softer, less accusatory. I raise my head and nod at her. I am glad too. The alternative is unthinkable.

Looking at her now, a full-grown person, I remember the first time I ever saw her. She wasn't breathing. Her eyes were wide open, black chasms of inscrutable depths. Her scrawny red body was stretched out impossibly long between the two gloved hands of the doctor, her head tilted just enough for her to make eye contact with me. She wasn't breathing. She looked right into my terrified eyes and did not blink. I remember thinking then that she was holding her breath.

As she grew, I never changed my mind. As she had resisted breathing, she resisted all things, withheld herself from me, kept unfathomable secrets that I yearned to know but was too afraid to ask.

Now here we are. She reaches for my face, and I pull away. I cling tightly to her hand, and she deftly slips it out of my grasp. We dance a painful pas de deux of need and regret, neither of us capable of anything more.

# On Shitting in the Woods and Other Tragedies of Running

*Scott F. Parker*

As all runners know, there are certain hazards that come with the territory. Among them: blisters, lost toenails, sweat-stained shirts, stinky socks, sore muscles and feet, aching knees and hips. Another hazard, bleeding—in most walks of life, as afflictions go, a rather glamorous one, suggesting profound heroism, desperate survival, or an expensive drug habit—for a runner, can be sourced to a range of dermal regions. Common are nipples, armpits, and inner thighs, none of which score well on the glamour scale. There is nothing romantic (certain fetishes possibly withstanding) about nipple blood. It is not the blood from sticker bush cuts, or from being hit by a car, or from falling down on rocks— proud, stalwart bloods, these, though surprisingly and disappointingly rare. No, nipple blood, armpit blood, inner thigh blood—the bloods I've bled—are distinctly pusillanimous and anemic. We runners do not bleed these bloods stoically. Rather we bleed them demonstrably and stingingly. The area of chafing in our inner thighs expands by the stride. The blood mixes with the sweat of our damp nethers, spreading itself in the pattern of uncollected menstrual blood. But our vital fluids aside, it is a solid that becomes liquid that is the momentous tragedy of running. The problems lie not in our circulatory or endocrine but in our digestive systems—that is, in our bowels.

The first time I had to shit on a run was probably the most embarrassing/traumatic/disgusting/illegal. I was doing a loop that was common for me during my early running years, down and around Laurelhurst Park. The park, about two miles from my parents' house, is the most remote point on the loop. It would be the most difficult locale from which to return home, bowels unmoved, should an emergency arise. And arise (or more accurately, descend), one day, one did.

I was approaching the park when I felt the rumblings in my intestines, bloated feelings followed by mysterious vacuous sensations as my running sloshed my guts. This lasted for a couple of blocks, as I tried to make rational arguments to my innards that they shouldn't be due for evacuation. Failing this tactic, I resorted to outright pleas for mercy: *Just wait till we get home and you can release whatever you want. I'll run slowly. I'll even walk*—squeezing tight and straining my face the whole way. But it was to no avail—my bowels proved stubborn, demanded evacuation, threatened explosion. Frantically, I sought refuge.

Laurelhurst is the kind of nice family park where people might picnic with their toddlers in the summer, feed the ducks in the spring, or now, it being a Saturday morning, walk their dogs. There are sections of tree coverage, particularly on the hill on the north side of the park, but walkers and other runners frequent the trails there. A park for privacy Laurelhurst is not.

Eventually (probably twenty or thirty seconds later, the way my mind, heart, and recesses were racing), I took cover in semi-obfuscating foliage and did my messy business. The release was a relief, but I wasn't out of the woods yet. I needed to clean up, and quickly, before someone's dog sniffed out my hiding spot. I tore some leaves off a bush and did my best, by which I mean that I sort of spread things around and ended up with some on my hand. Thoroughly disgusted, and more thoroughly embarrassed, I emerged slowly and casually. No one was around. Now to get home invisibly. I wanted to run to be there sooner, but I wasn't confident that I could without triggering another release, so I walked, quickly when I could, squeezingly when I had to. I took side streets when possible—but would have to come out to cross the freeway at 28th—so as to decrease the chances that someone from my high school would drive by and see me covered in shit, as I imagined myself to be. I had made it inconspicuously across Burnside back to Northeast Portland when I noticed a red sedan coming my way. It looked familiar. It couldn't be. But there it was. I made out the distinctive missing side-view mirror of my aunt's car. *Should I flag her down for a ride? Tell her what is going on and pray for familial pity and discretion?* No. It was too embarrassing. *Pretend nothing is the matter, that I am just out looking for a ride?* No, she'd smell me out. I took cover again, now behind a telephone pole, hoping I hadn't already been seen. It worked. She passed, and I made it home to a toilet, a shower, and a garbage can for my briefs.

Subsequently, I've avoided such horrifying experiences. I ascribe my success to two factors: skill and luck.

The skill is one that I learned from Uncle Joe. One morning at the beach he returned from a run and jocularly motioned for me to look at his feet—not his yellowing fungus-infected toes; his shoes still covered them—but above his shoe-line, at his mismatched ankles: one socked, the other not. He pointed this out to me in particular, assuming that I, a runner, would make the proper induction as to the reasoning behind his peculiar dress. He didn't realize that I was unfamiliar with the single-socked runner and had not yet learned one of running's fundamental rules. It was too obvious to think to point out. Yet somehow, in the bushes of Laurelhurst Park, I had failed to figure it out for myself: socks offer sturdier wiping, more even spread, and better absorption than tree leaves. In retrospect, I add an absence of ingenuity to my embarrassments.

And though it is humbling to reveal one's ignorance, it is a sign of wisdom to learn from our mistakes and be willing to consider new ideas in our lives. Pooping has really brought this home for me. Many times, post epiphany, I have returned from a run and proudly gestured to my own mismatched ankles. My girlfriend, whether consciously or not, has developed the habit of surveying my feet whenever she sees me finish a run. Occasionally, I'll return sockless and she'll ask me what happened. My response is either that I drank too much coffee or that I forgot to wear socks, a careless mistake every time it's made, considering all the benefits derived from these cotton sacks.

*Socks offer sturdier wiping, more even spread, and better absorption than tree leaves.*

Luck has complemented this important running skill for me too. As resourceful a sock-skill as I've developed, I'd still rather not have to use it. Of course that's not realistic for me. Shitting is part of running. I take what precautionary measures I can by consciously trying to go before a run and not running immediately after a lot of coffee, but occasionally shit still happens. My luck has been that it has always happened somewhere safe-ish. Knock on wood—I have not had to shit in as public a place as Laurelhurst Park again. No, every time this issue has, so to say, stuck its head out, I've been in a remote forest—my old socks are buried all over Forest Park—or within holding-it distance of a Port-O-Potty.

Unfortunately, Port-O-Potties scare me.[1] And it is only in a quasi-emergency that I'll use one—I much prefer the forest. But as these quasi-emergencies continue to haunt me, my resistance to the Port-O-Potty is breaking down. My most recent excretory incident involves a Port-O-Potty and a dose of embarrassment, though not of the I've-just-shit-myself-in-the-middle-of-a-race variety.[2]

---

1 Not just Port-O-Potties but all manner of public toilets. In high school I used to skip class and go home—sometimes run home—rather than go at school.

2 This does happen. In the 2007 Portland Marathon I passed a runner who had done just that. From a distance it looked like an unusual tattoo. It wasn't until I was directly behind him that I could tell that he had shat himself. Diarrhea ran all down his legs to his socks, which were, it should be noted, quite absorptive. That this runner did not drop out of the race, as some spectators seemed to think he should, earns him a great deal of my respect. If I ever don't make it to that Port-O-Potty, I hope I have the courage to run like he did.

Here's how that incident went. I had just moved back to Portland from Korea and hadn't run in months. My sister, Coach, asked me if I wanted to run a 10K with her. I did. The morning of the race, still under the effects of jet lag, I woke up to eat breakfast early enough to not have a full stomach for the race, and to drink coffee early enough to not have a full anything else during the race. But I horribly mistimed everything and was just pouring my coffee when Coach came to pick me up. Against my better judgment, I took the coffee with me in the car and drank it on the way to the race. The race started fine. My legs felt good, despite the long break. My stomach was okay; the cup of coffee had only been about twelve ounces. Coach and I ran together at about a 7:45 pace for a couple of miles. Comfortable for me. A nice welcome-back-to-Portland run with my sister.

Then it hit me.

The unabsorbed coffee gurgled in my stomach. I thought to myself, *Good thing it's only four more miles or I'd be in some trouble*. Then I felt the sinking feeling deeper down that signals, *Four miles or not, you are in trouble*. I checked my socks—missing. Under the thinking that it was *only a 10K*, I hadn't worn any. I said, "Coach, give me your socks."

She said, "You're an idiot. These socks cost ten bucks."

"I'll buy you new socks. Just give me those ones."

"No. Use your own socks."

"I don't have any."

"Tough."

"Come on, Coach."

"Nope. Ha ha."[3]

Suddenly, every running stride had a chance of release. I slowed to a barely jogging pace. Coach went ahead. I looked around for a tree, hoping to abandon my shirt this time and make it out okay. As fate would have it, we were in country fields. There was no cover to be sought. I started panicking. There was a house ahead. I wondered if they would let me use their bathroom. But their BEWARE OF DOGS sign kept me from asking. I slowed further, alternating between squeezing my sphincter hard for a few walking steps and running for as many steps as I could string together before I was certain I was going to brown my shorts. Praying for a simple tree, I was given a Port-O-Potty ahead at the turnaround. Coach passed me on her way back to the finish. I threw my unneeded shirt at her head and jogged gingerly to the toilet. I had the fortune of being the first runner to shit there that morning, so it smelled okay and looked clean inside. Still, I squatted above

---

3    She really said, "Ha ha." Not to make her look bad, though; she
     wouldn't say that to anyone except me—and possibly Cousin Steve.

the seat, making sure not to make contact with the surface. This concerned me at first—I didn't want to exhaust my legs in the middle of a race—until I admitted how horribly the race was going regardless. I ran better on the way back but still lost to Coach by several minutes, something she still mocks me about.

In the spirit of healthy fraternal jest, I often attempt to mock Coach in return. Sadly for me, runners' excretions are not limited to solid waste (even if it's not necessarily all that solid). We have to pee too. And while this has never troubled me much—I had to stop and pee after the first mile of my first marathon, but that was because I was so paranoid about dehydration that I couldn't stop chugging water, even while standing at the starting line—most of Coach's stories are of this number, making them by necessity less mockable. By chance, her stories are also infinitely cooler.

A brief Hood to Coast (H2C) interpolation is called for. H2C is the relay race that puts twelve-member teams in two vans at Timberline Lodge on Mount Hood and has them run almost two hundred miles to the beach. Some of these teams are made up of fast runners who cover the course in under twenty hours. Some teams are made up of runners who cover the course in twenty to twenty-five hours. Other teams are made up of people who like

sweating without showering and want to find out how good beer can taste after staying up twenty-four hours, giving themselves blisters and cramps while running, and cramming into vans.

With friends we put a team together whenever we can. H2C is an absurdly popular race. Every year registration is capped at one thousand teams, and every year five hundred more than that sign up on the first day of registration, ten months before the race. Allegedly, a raffle determines who gets to pay $1,000+ to run this race, but to anyone who's paying attention, the Gonads team has had an improbable run of luck.

Our teams are usually a combination of the fast-but-not-especially-so type of runner and the type who are primarily interested in beer. Our fastest team ran in 2002. It was Coach's first year on the team. We were consistently beating our projected times. This, coupled with bad cell phone coverage in the Coastal Mountains, made it exceedingly difficult to coordinate meeting times between vans. (Each team's vans leapfrog one another. One van of people goes ahead to rest, while the other van's members run about a thirty- to thirty-five-mile section of the course.) While the runners in Coach's van were running their second set of legs, the runners in my van were sleeping in a field. Our alarms were set for six thirty a.m. That would give us forty-five minutes to wake up and drive the mile down the road to where Coach would hand the bracelet off to our first runner, Courtney. At six a.m., the sun rising, Cousin Brian and I couldn't sleep. To take advantage of the downtime, we started cleaning out the van, throwing out Power Bar wrappers and smelly socks. The garbage can was a hundred yards away, across the field, along the road where runners were passing by. We walked stiffly—our legs slow to loosen from the cramped hours in the van and short nap in the grass—toward it. As we neared, I joked to Cousin Brian, "That looks a lot like my sister's stride."

He, with the better eye, confirmed the stride. "Holy shit, it is her!"

By then Coach was there and saw us standing around like fools. "What the hell are you guys doing? You better be there when I finish!"

"Well, slow down then."

"No! You hurry up!"

"We gotta move!"

We ran back across the field, shouting to our slumbering vanmates. "Get up. Coach is here. We gotta go. Courtney, get your shoes on."

We hustled as well as we could, pulled out of the field onto the road, and chased Coach. We passed her with almost half a mile left for her to run, yelling out the window for her to slow down. The rage in her glare chilled us. We raced on. With luck we could have four minutes to get Courtney dressed and to the starting line.

Then we stopped the van. The end of leg twenty-four is one of the big exchange points. Both vans from each team gather there for van #1 runners to begin their final legs. The parking lot was a mess. We waited in line on the highway to get to the turn-off. Coach was gaining on us. We wouldn't make it in time. Courtney and I jumped out of the van and ran ahead to the starting line. She had her shoes on and tied by now. That would have to be enough. I had the watch and clipboard to record the time of the exchange. As we came into the madness of the exchange point and got Courtney into the chute, we heard Coach coming in shouting: "Courtney! Where the hell are you?"

Courtney waved an arm, accepted the slap-bracelet, and was off. Coach, meanwhile, still looked pissed. I said, "Nice running. You guys came in way fast again."

Hands on head, between gasps, she barked out to no one in particular, "Watch out. Coming through. I peed my pants."

By then her vanmates had gathered around us. "You pissed yourself. Why?"

"I had to go. Didn't wanna stop. What else was I supposed to do?"

"How much came out? Like just a few drops?"

"No, a full pee. I didn't have time to make it to a Port-O-Potty before I started."

It's difficult to express how cool we thought that was, so we nodded, registering her urine as a definitive statement of her heroism and, by association, confirmation of how badass we were. It represented everything we wanted to stand for as runners. We looked down at the evidence on her legs. They were wet. It looked like sweat, but given the circumstances, who could tell? Within minutes, as the story spread among our camp, I noticed other runners taking extra sips of water, hoping to have the chance to prove themselves similarly.

And while no one else peed themselves, the overly liquid-filled stomachs may have contributed to one of H2C's distinctive characteristics: runners' runs—my last scatological topic. Based on years of observation, the bowel movements produced during H2C seem to be marked by a surprising uniformity.

Plato's theory of forms supposes a perfect and transcendent form to physical objects. The chairs that we sit in are imitations, imperfect replications, of the ideal chair. You wouldn't expect an ideal conical poo, but if Plato is to be followed, there must be one. And H2C effectively requires its participants to model this unusual form.

These deep brown and occasionally green-highlighted cones build during H2C on a bed of saturated toilet paper thick enough to support up to a pound of weight. The conical shape isn't intuitive. It has to do with the texture of the material. The combination of running, Power Bars, and too much water tends to soften things, but not in the extreme case as with coffee, grease, etc. This peculiar and very particular form of excrement is most commonly found in Port-O-Potties between Government Camp and downtown Portland. It is in this stretch that the above factors are frequently added to the compounding variables: heat and nerves. There is a lot of excitement in the buildup to H2C. For most who do it—some people find sitting in a shit-stinking van with cramped muscles for a day and a half an experience not worth repeating (H2Cers consider these people strange.)—H2C is one of the highlights of the running year, if not the year itself. The annual hullabaloo is my guess as to why so many runners, after their first legs, legs that on their own aren't much different from regular training runs, run straight through the exchange points and to the bathrooms. On training runs we don't get nervous, psyche ourselves out, over-hydrate, or run too fast trying to impress our friends.

As for the mess of the rest, as runners adapt to the environment between Portland and Seaside, bowel movements become more sporadic and tailor to the idiosyncrasies of individual digestive tracts and diets.

Some people need to go constantly. Others don't go again until the race is over. But lines for Port-O-Potties remain long, and thick viscous cones remain common. A reliable, if not entirely comforting, sight and reminder of the range of running's effects.

Of course there are other perils that plague runners, and I've had them all: hit by car, lost, scared of dark, strangers, red face, penile shrinkage, tight hamstrings. But compared to the adversities of the innards, to this runner, these do not seem so formidable. That's easy for me to say. The majority of my collisions with cars have been initiated by me in misguided attempts to prove some kind of unarticulated moral point to the drivers—and none of them have been at all serious. Being lost is more fun than it sounds, assuming, as has always been the case for me, you eventually become un-lost. Being scared of the dark helps you run faster. Red face can be remedied with a cold shower; shrinkage with a warm one; tight hamstrings with yoga. These are emboldening obstacles. You can run through them all (as long as you instigated the car collision)—and the harder you do, the better. Pooping, however, is cowering. And cowardice is what we run to escape. That the very emotion we are running away from is built (maybe not for all runners, but for me apparently) into the essence of that escape makes the act self-defeating. Unless running also offers a deeper retreat from the ethereal and anesthetized conceptions of what we would like our bodies to be, toward a real and human acceptance of what they are: highly sophisticated shit-making machines.

# I've Been to Jero Tapakan

*Cecilie Scott*

Three weeks into summer quarter, the Seattle weather warmed enough for tank tops and sleeveless blouses. We were all from elsewhere, friends because each day we struggled to learn Bahasa Indonesia and, like travelers, we were free to touch on tender subjects. None of the women beneath the cherry tree would have mentioned my asymmetry earlier but, once exposed, the inky wave that curled over the tip of my shoulder was itself a legitimate topic of curiosity.

"A tattoo—instead of reconstruction?"

"I didn't want any more surgery. And the mastectomy left me with a smooth, wide slate."

"When was the surgery?"

"Almost two years ago now, between my first and second trips to Bali."

"And the tattoo?"

"Last winter, only the outlines so far. Madame Lazonga says she'll need at least two more sessions to color it in."

Cancer talk draws fear; I felt it sidle into place, just beyond our circle. I was, and still am, learning to make it welcome, rendering it a more homely presence.

"My grandfather died from cancer this spring," said Dewi, a visiting instructor from Java with smooth skin and long black, shining hair. She was the youngest woman among us that day. Indonesian teacher-student etiquette is formal, but because we weren't her students—she taught the other beginners' class—she could lounge on the grass with us without risking impropriety.

We murmured sympathy, and Gloria—the weathered blonde from Florida who'd already won our admiration as a free-spirited traveler learning a new language for fun (no grad school ambitions)—asked, "Did they find the cancer too late for treatment?"

Dewi paused for a moment before she said, "We all die someday."

We were silent for a heartbeat or two, glancing from Dewi to Gloria, eyes sliding past eyes in our discomfort.

Dewi continued, "From the outside, the money Americans spend on individual patients seems strange when you do not give health care to everyone."

"Yes, our maternal and infant mortality rates are shameful," Lynn, tall and earnest, from New York and The New School, was the first to agree. But then, we were all ready to accept Dewi's criticism as

part of our cross-cultural learning. Underlying all
the practical considerations of the language program
was the passion we shared for learning about other
lives and cultures, a passion that kept us muttering
in response to tapes in the language lab, in dorm
rooms, or at home, and—in my case—on the long
drive to Seattle from the Cascade foothills.

Dewi's statement brought us around a full 180
degrees to face our own assumptions about death.
In the United States, we will admit (when pressed)
that all must die someday, but we have a hard time
accepting this. We praise cancer patients for their
struggle to survive, and we act as cheerleaders
throughout that struggle. We quote Dylan Thomas
at every opportunity: "Do not go gentle into that
good night / Rage, rage against the dying of the
light." As the expectation that cancer is treatable
becomes part of popular culture, a diagnosis of
cancer is no longer a death foretold but merely a
gypsy's warning, heeded only by the faint of heart.
The ideal cancer patient is a fearless survivor, while
the rest of us fall short.

By the time I sat with those women beneath
the cherry tree, I had come to think of cancer as a
teacher. The first lesson I'd learned was that I could
die—not would, but *could*. Knowing that death was
possible had freed me to learn more because it lifted
the here and now into high relief. Of course, it was

easier to be positive nineteen months after surgery and a succession of reassuring mammograms, blood tests, and breast exams. I knew I was lucky: my cancer was at a manageable stage, I had complete insurance coverage through my husband's union, and good medical care was available.

Antioch University Seattle is small—minuscule when compared to the University of Washington. It's far from, and fairly independent of, the original Antioch College in Yellow Springs, Ohio. Those of us working toward a master's degree in Whole Systems Design (WSD) were in its smallest program. Nevertheless, I was part of a cluster of breast cancer survivors there. Elaine, the faculty member who had led the university's first study abroad, the Bali trip, was a down-winder. She and her sister had both been exposed to fallout in Utah, both of them had had

breast cancer, and only Elaine survived. Donna, a former airline flight attendant, a master's student, and now the BA program assistant, had been under forty when her first breast cancer was found. This was followed by a second cancer in that breast, but Donna survived both rounds, becoming an expert on biopsies and lumpectomies. Jann, another WSD student, had been diagnosed with breast cancer the year after I was. She traveled to Bali with Antioch's second Bali group a few months later and centered her intercultural studies on healing. According to Jann, cancer was a verb. Her response: "I don't do that anymore."

Jann joked we were a perfect pair, one left breast and one right between us. We'd each worn our mastectomy bras, equipped with prostheses, during our separate stays in Bali, passing for normal there—or as normal as possible for outsized, red-faced Westerners among a compact, pale-brown people. Back in Seattle, we bitched about brassieres that couldn't support one breast without the counterweight of a silicon slab in the second pouch.

"I tried adhesive tape today, but it pulled loose," Jann said, tugging down one side of her bra. "This damn thing's trying to strangle me!" Proudly unreconstructed, she loved my tattoo but wasn't ready to settle on a single image. The women's restroom was an impromptu showroom where she

modeled each temporary tattoo—roses or twining
vines or a gorgeous hummingbird. "How about this
one?" she'd ask. We mirrored each other's wicked
grins the week she'd applied a wolf, teeth bared, to
the white space above her left ribs.

"No more cancer or cancering," Jann said. "I've
been to Jero Tapakan."

*Jero* is an honorary Balinese title: a *balian* has a
special relationship with the spirit world, and a
*balian tapakan* is a traditional healer who calls upon
the spirit world to help his or her clients. Has the
family van thrown a rod? Does your grandson lie
listless with a low-grade fever? Is your orange grove
afflicted with a white powder, the once-green leaves
lying shriveled on the ground? Something is out of
balance, possibly through witchcraft, so it makes
sense to visit a balian who can channel the spirit
of a departed ancestor to speak to you directly and
tell you what steps you must take to restore the
necessary equilibrium. Although Balinese aren't
convinced that the ancestors of Westerners can be
called all the way to Bali, healers are willing to try,
adapting the tools of their art—magical oils, chants,
and music—to invite spirits to aid foreign clients.

Yes, we all must die in time, but meanwhile it's
prudent to ask for whatever help we can get. And
so, Jann had hired a driver with a van for the trip to
Jero Tapakan's remote village.

I'd also met Jero Tapakan. On my first visit to
Bali, our guide I Wayan Budiasa (Budi) took us into
the hills of Gianyar for a meeting with the balian.
After a long drive over steep and twisting mountain
roads, we stopped at a village so our driver could
ask around for directions. Soon we were at a small
house compound at the end of a narrow street. We
stood behind a group of about twenty Balinese

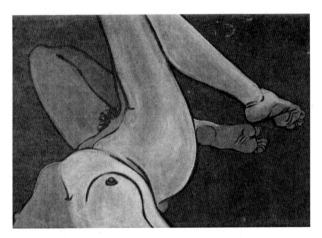

sitting, squatting, or kneeling on the ground before
an open doorway. A middle-age woman knelt upon
a platform within the dim room, speaking with
a masculine voice. Budi explained that she was
speaking in trance with the voice of an ancestor, the
uncle of a woman who knelt directly in front of the

platform. This woman had come for help and now listened intently, supported by a group of family members. The other Balinese were observers too, but their turn to call upon an ancestor would come. After a while our guide signaled us to back out. This was not the balian tapakan we sought. We were getting closer, though. Our driver had found the route to a nearby village where another healer lived and practiced.

Again, our small bus climbed and dipped and turned along narrow roads until it pulled up in a village that looked to us exactly like the one we'd left. This time we filed into a larger courtyard. Budi performed the introductions, leading Elaine and Colleen (working on her master's thesis about modes of alternative healing) to the veranda.

Jero Tapakan was simply dressed in a blue cotton blouse and a sarong wrapped around her thick waist, stopping just above her broad bare feet. Her hair was pulled back from a high forehead and gathered in a neat bun at the back of her round head. After seating Elaine and Colleen on either side of her and talking with them briefly, she nodded to Budi who took his place in front of the veranda so he could translate and be heard across the small courtyard to the *bale*, an open pavilion where the rest of us perched, a row of brightly colored birds along its edge. Trudi, a young MA student who was determined to miss nothing, seemed positioned for flight at the end of the row. I sat next to her, notebook open and pen ready.

We were wrapped in our new sarongs, proper dress for formal calls and temple visits. After a week in Bali, we knew enough to keep our sandal-shod feet on the ground and to remove our shoes before stepping into any building. We could also make the distinction between the plain concrete slab that served most Balinese for an everyday floor and the red-tiled floor which raised the status of this bale above the ordinary.

Clearly, Jero Tapakan was accustomed to telling her story to visitors, and what followed was a set piece, broken into short sections for ease of translation. Budi turned first-person narrative to third person and, as I dutifully transcribed his words, I recognized the outline of a classic folktale. You know how it goes—the destitute protagonist sets out on a journey and along the way receives a magical device from a stranger. Despite obstacles and temptations, she returns home to rejection and disbelief, but learns to use the power of this gift:

*She became Jero Tapakan because the tradition was in her family.*

*But before she became Jero Tapakan, she and her husband were poor, and she earned money as a traveling peddler. Her baby was sick. They had many debts, and their creditors were pressing. She fled into the forest, planning to kill herself, but drew back in fear that her spirit would be punished. She walked on until she came to a village where the people took pity on her and asked her to stay. On her way home to bring her husband back to work on this new land, she met a peddler with a white eel for sale. She bargained for and bought it—a white eel with a mustache.*

*Now as she was walking along, someone asked her why she carried this poisonous fish that was no good to eat. He offered to buy it for a high price, one hundred times more than she had paid for it. But when she told him she was not bargaining, she turned her head to see him, and he was gone. She knew then that she had been talking with a spirit.*

*When she got home she cooked the eel in coconut oil, although the people said it was poisonous. She saved the oil in a bottle for three days, and the people told her she was crazy. So the* agung *(village head) came to her and told her she must leave.*

The story continued and rejection changed to recognition as she learned the power of the magic oil and accepted her calling as a balian who could call up spirits while in a trance. I didn't doubt the contents of Jero Tapakan's story just because its form was common. And we wouldn't have been there that day if she hadn't become a well-known and widely respected balian. I was intrigued, though, by the human need to select from our experiences those elements we can use to tell a story, a way of making a whole from fragments.

I grew up hearing stories of healing, each shaped to illustrate the tenets of Christian Science: sickness and death are but errors in thought. These were more amiable certainties than the ones delivered in our Lutheran pastor's Sunday sermons when I was twelve: stories shaped to convince his flock that hell awaits all sinners—and we were all sinners.

Trudi and I lost track of Jero Tapakan's chronicle when Nyoman, her assistant, sat down on the edge of the bale, tucking herself between us. A matter-of-fact woman of about thirty, Nyoman had heard Jero Tapakan's story many times by now. She was curious about us: "Where are you from?" "Are you married?" "How many children do you have?" she asked in Bahasa Indonesia. By then we recognized these standard questions and could answer and ask her the same in return. Trudi pulled out her favorite phrase book, and the three of us passed it back and forth, rummaging for words to keep the conversation going. Nyoman showed us a small photo album, displaying pictures of Jero Tapakan with other visitors and pointing with pride to Linda Connor, one of the anthropologists who'd made an ethnographic film of Jero Tapakan in a trance session. Before we left, Trudi took pictures, promising to send prints for their album.

Our whole group lined up along the path to the spirit gate in the wall that separated the compound from the road. Jero Tapakan walked along, smiling warmly at each of us as she shook our hands—until she came to me. As she started to shake my hand, grasping my right arm with her left hand, she paused, moved her right hand up my arm, and then frowned and shook her head. I was curious but not alarmed. After we'd clambered back on the bus, Trudi—ever the Elephant's Child—asked Budi, "What was that all about? Why did Jero stop in front of Cecilie? Why did she shake her head like that?" Budi looked at me, looked away, and shrugged his shoulders. I didn't press for a better answer—I didn't want one. I wrote the question in my notes for that day, and then forgot about it until a biopsy of my right breast found cancer five months later. I believe Jero Tapakan sensed something wrong when her hand grasped my arm. I didn't know if her powers reached past perception, but when Jann turned to Jero Tapakan for a healing ceremony, I understood why.

Friday afternoons were slow in the computer lab, so I was alone in the university basement when Jann stopped by, our first chance for a good visit since she'd got back from Bali. Jann told me then about the ceremony held for her, setting the scene so I could picture Jero Tapakan's tile-floored pavilion.

At one end, a gamelan gong ensemble knelt before their instruments and played. At the other end, a table held bottles of medicine and baskets filled with offerings for the gods, all waiting to be blessed when Jero Tapakan lit the incense that would carry her prayers upward. And in the middle, there was Jann, stripped down to a sarong and lying on a mat.

*Another world*, I thought, rolling my chair farther back from keyboard and screen.

Jann continued her story from her seat at the end of a silent row of Macs. "There I was, bare-naked above the waist. Jero began rubbing me down with that magic coconut oil. Good thing I'd worn panties because she undid my sarong and oiled my legs as well. Meanwhile the gong was gonging and someone was chanting. You know how it is. Sometimes you can't tell where the sound of the gamelan ends and the singing starts. It all blurs together, and you get dizzy if you try to sort it out."

"And people in the courtyard?"

"Standing room only. I was part of the show."

"Not an easy way to satisfy that part of the course, the experiential learning requirement."

"No, but I didn't have to take a dance class. Or gamelan lessons." Jann brightened and grinned. "I was basted, chanted over, and rewrapped in my sarong, this time up to my armpits. Then Jero's assistant led me back to my room."

"How were you after all that?"

"I don't know. I was out of it. But I slept for sixteen hours!" Jann started laughing. "There is power there. I could feel it. But I really amazed Jero the next morning, just before I left. I was all properly dressed for Ubud, complete with two boobs. Jero reached out and touched them. She thought that the healing had worked immediately and that I'd sprouted a new breast overnight. I showed her the prosthesis, and she smiled and laughed at herself before hugging me goodbye."

Although many Balinese believe it is dangerous to talk about witchcraft and magic for fear of offending even the most benign balian or wizard, Jero Tapakan worked within a web of magic, traditional herbalism, and Western medicine. In Bali, there seems to be no need to accept only one system. A person will go to a doctor for injections, plaster her forehead with a poultice of herbs when she has a headache, and see a balian for a life-threatening illness, all the while maintaining balance with daily offerings and prayers.

I thought of Jann's visit to Jero Tapakan when Dewi said, "We all die someday." Sitting there beneath the cherry trees, Lynn, Gloria, and I had willingly suspended disbelief, accepting for a moment that some-where, perhaps in Indonesia, a group of people saw death as a part of life. We wanted an alternative to the denial of death we'd grown up with. Although cultural assumptions can shape

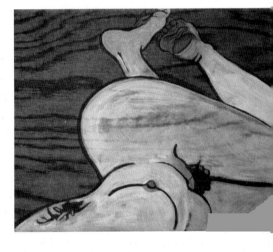

the way we express this, denial isn't learned—it's a gut-level response. Wherever possible, in the United States and in Bali, we visit doctors and healers accompanied by family members and friends. We ask, *Why me?* We take moral inventories. We grasp at medicine and magic.

Jann could handle a mastectomy. "That was cut and run!" she said. But she looked for alternatives to standard medicine as practiced by the doctors on her health plan because she valued her life. "The surgeon thought I was a smartass. Two weeks after the mastectomy, he showed me how to make tiny little circles with my arm extended. 'Oh,' I said, 'so I can do this.' And I put my arm straight up into the air over my head. Childish showing off, I know, but it felt good! Less vulnerable." Jann had already learned that exercising right away after mastectomy was necessary to maintain a full range of motion and to help prevent lymphedema. She couldn't trust a doctor who'd neglected to tell her this.

Before Jann traveled to Bali, she dropped by the computer lab to talk about the results of her lymph node staging. "Only a couple of nodes were positive." Not good news, because in the world of cancer testing, positive is bad; test results don't report healthy cells, only deviations. (I'd bawled in relief when I learned my lymph nodes were negative.)

"They want to give me chemo," she said. "I told them no. I don't have cancer."

"But your lymph nodes?"

"That only means cells were found. No tumor, no growth. Oh, I know cells can spread and multiply. But they don't know why some do and some don't. So they want to poison me, just in case."

"Your cancer was estrogen positive?"

"Yes—they were willing to compromise. Offered Tamoxifen, while they wear me down. But that's still treating a cancer I don't have."

At times it feels easier to fight doctors than to face cancer, especially when your doctors see your body as a war zone. "I'm getting calls from different doctors," Jann told me a couple of weeks later. "Scary calls. And the office visits. They give me graphic details on the horrible deaths of women with breast cancer."

Jann had already been threatened with the horrors of hell and damnation, threats that continued well past childhood. "For twenty years I bounced back and forth between praying and cursing, never knowing which was doing me the most good, but aware that 'my father in heaven' didn't respond to either in any way I could see." She was her own woman by the time I met her, and she was prepared to question all authority. "I tell my doctor, 'I don't have cancer.' He says, 'Yes you do,' and shakes his finger in my face. I try to tell him how I feel about the various treatments, traditional and alternative. 'Feelings don't count,' he says. 'Statistics do.' I tell him I'm not a statistic. 'You're going to be,' he says, getting in the last word."

Instead, Jann went to Jero Tapakan, saw an Ayurvedic doctor who shared meals once a month with his patients so they'd learn how to buy and cook healthy foods, and worked with a naturopathic group. "These doctors greet me with adult language. They say, 'How are you?' instead of using *we*—as if this disease is an equally shared experience. God, that pisses me off!" And she sought sources of women's power, entering a PhD program at Union Institute to study cultures that honored the goddess.

"No more cancer or cancering," she said. She found an oncologist willing to treat her on her terms—diagnosis and support, advice without threats—because those cancer cells did coalesce and grow. I doubt the doctor had any illusions as to the outcome. A tumor was found in her brain, and she canceled her trip to Ireland. She agreed to the proposed radiation, but concentrated on visualization until the tumor shrank enough to end her headaches and thus the need for surgery.

Three of us, old friends from the university, visited Jann one afternoon. In emerald green velour that brought out the red in her hair, Jann sat on the couch, her color good and her hair thick. She told us what happened when the hospice worker showed up at her door. "I said she was mistaken. So she looked on her clipboard and assured me that my name was down as needing hospice care. I thought I was being polite, but our dog must have picked up on my vibes. He raced out of the house and ran her off."

"Rexie couldn't have done her any harm," Jann's sister-in-law laughed as she brought in a tray of tea and cookies. "He's completely toothless."

The next time I saw her, Jann was using the oxygen tank on loan from hospice. Cancer had spread to her lungs. No morphine dulled the pain or clouded her mind. "I'll be ready to let go," she said. "Soon."

I think Jann could have worked with an oncologist from the beginning, if she'd found one reckless enough to work with her. Doctors who let their patients set treatment boundaries risk charges of malpractice, and Jann wouldn't have turned her life over to anyone. Much as I miss her, I can't see death as her failure. Even obedient and compliant cancer patients die.

Magic and medicine offer to save us from disease, impairment, and death, and we accept their gifts whenever we can. We resist death, no matter the religious lessons we are taught to explain it or to ease our dying.

When Dewi told us that her grandfather accepted death, I remembered my own father, fed by a stomach tube and aware only of his bodily sensations, a fretful infant at seventy-eight but still holding fast to life. I didn't seek out Jero Tapakan on my second trip to Bali. Instead, I turned to meditation. Maybe by the time my death arrives, I'll be able to let go.

# On Leaving Home
*Sandra Arguello*

## Act I

The scene around me is exactly how I recall my town's market thirty years ago when my mother would take me shopping for vegetables and meat: the same not-so-fresh fish suspiciously staring from its ice cage, the smell of thick tortillas made by chubby ladies in green aprons, and the voices of sweaty men calling us "queen" or "princess" or "love" as they leer. Only now such attention does not bother me. I am at an age when a little male attention, even from strangers, is flattering. But today, the old man sitting next to me at this *soda* in Heredia's main market just wants some conversation.

"Nothing is like it used to be," he says, watching disapprovingly as two teenagers walk by in very short skirts. "In my time women were more decent."

I wonder if I will get to the point where I find myself disapprovingly saying, "Nothing is like in Costa Rica." Many things aren't. That is the magic of moving away.

To some people here at home, I seem crazy: to start school again at thirty-eight in a foreign country when most women my age are raising kids and worrying about mortgages, husbands, and prosperous careers. I feel like Odysseus, on a voyage to fight some wars, though mine are mostly internal. I am hoping to finally find out who I really am.

I am spending my last morning in Costa Rica at this market because I want to capture one smell that I have found only in Third-World countries: public imperfection. It rises from the floor and slowly climbs around everything it finds, like a creeper. It is not exactly the smell of poverty. Rather, it epitomizes a lifestyle based on the idea of time as a friend who brings joy, not as an enemy to be fought and conquered.

Everything about the market could be better. The floor could be cleaner. The cloth to clean the tables could be whiter. The hands of the ladies making tortillas could be less greasy. But time is precious because it means enjoying one more conversation, one more smile with a stranger, or one more bit of gossip about the neighbor's new lover. For Costa Ricans, born and raised in the *pura vida* land, time used to perfect the details of life is wasted time.

The old man sitting next to me happens to be called Jesús, as many of his contemporaries are. After five minutes, I know about his family and life as if he were an acquaintance of many years. The hot coffee makes him sweat; he takes out a worn, yellowish handkerchief from his pocket and wipes the drops on his forehead. He puts it on the counter, where customers before him have placed coins, bills, dirty napkins.

Hard work, dust, crowded places, and sweating bodies: these are the smells of public imperfection and of the sense of community so ingrained in our Latin American countries.

There is a sunburned tourist with an expensive camera trying to take home the look of the exotic, of this otherness that is at the root of so many cultural misunderstandings. We are probably a colorful scene for a postcard: two dark-skinned people drinking coffee from glasses and eating cheese *empanadas.*

I often think about what I will look like in Portland, my soon-to-be new home. I am not the type of foreigner that makes a newspaper story. I am not an undocumented alien, desperate to send money home, learning new tricks to fool the *migra.* I will not be risking my life sailing for days on a boat to Florida. There is no language barrier. Still, I will be foreign.

It does not rain as I walk out of the market with a bag of coffee and mixed feelings of joy and nostalgia, characteristic of those who are about to leave. In my handbag rests a plane ticket to the USA, the

promised land for so many before and after me.
Return date: open.

# Act II

Airports are weird. They offer the first impressions
of a place, yet everything is transitional and fast.
After a stopover in Houston, the Portland airport
seems welcoming enough. It is not just the change
in temperature that tells me I am finally away from

home. As soon as I step out, there it is, the smell of the First World: plastic—hygienic, clean, safe.

I can't choose how to spend my first day in the United States. (America, for those of us below the border, is the whole continent. I find it funny when people ask me, "How long have you been in America?" I've never left! I've lived on the American continent all my life.) Marcela is a Costa Rican I met through the Internet, and she's agreed to help me out during my first days here. The local culture is already part of her life, and she's forgotten what time means for us, filling my day with a to-do list: open a bank account, go grocery shopping, check in with the university. All I want to do is walk around and feel the new air and assimilate the new smells.

"Costa Rica! How nice to live on an island," the blond teller at the bank says.

"I am not from Puerto Rico," I am used to explaining. Costa Rica is a tiny country in Central America and for us (the so-called representatives of Democracy in Latin America) the mistake is a painful one that shows how insignificant we can be in the world. So I am beginning to feel invisible. It is a feeling of new freedom I need to get used to. I come from a town where the grocery store owner carried me as a baby. Too much familiarity can spoil you. You feel too safe in your little world. It turns out that Rebecca, the blond bank teller, does not know if I can open an account with my foreign passport. In her thirty-something years, she has never had a passport herself—I forgive her for the geographical mistake.

It is at a supermarket on my first day in Portland that I miss my city for the first time. I miss that smell of imperfection. At Fred Meyer, I encounter what epitomizes the USA for many Latin Americans: organized, clean aisles full of too many brands of a single item. Choices. So many choices make me anxious. Which brand of soap should I buy? I don't even understand why we need so many! As anyone on a budget, I go for the cheapest. I remember the Dalai Lama saying that he likes supermarkets because they are full of beautiful, colorful things he does not need. It is this abundance of the First World that compels many immigrants to come here, to leave behind the stain of lack. "A stain," my ninety-nine-year-old auntie used to say, "that does not go away, not even with bleach."

*I miss that smell of imperfection.*

Here, people seem to both worship and fear time. While I grew up in a culture that accepts leaving something for tomorrow, or the day after, I now find myself in a culture where every minute counts. Doors that glide as you walk through them. Machines that sell train tickets. Toilets that flush before you are ready. Automatic soap dispensers. Vending machines. This automation represents an interesting concept: life must be made easier in order to use time for more important tasks, like say, succeeding. But it also means less human contact and old trades

that are lost. In some towns in Costa Rica, there are still some specimens of a dying, peculiar occupation: toilet paper sellers at public restrooms. Scarcity calls for imagination.

As I get into bed my first night, I feel tired but excited. After all, I have many acts to add to this story. Life, as they say, has just begun.

# Act III

It's finally summer in Portland, nine months after my arrival. I take a look back and see myself a little differently. I've come to appreciate automatic doors as I carry my groceries home. I walk the aisles at Fred Meyer, and I already know where to find my favorite soap. In some ways I blend in—but I am still a foreigner, and I like this. I am exotic but not alone. It is true that the USA is a melting pot; I have met people from more nationalities in these past months than in my whole life back in Costa Rica.

The Odysseus in me has made it to a safe land. There is always something new to discover, which keeps my life interesting. Yet it is also reassuring to feel the familiarity of my new home. Last week somebody stopped me on the street to ask for directions. And I knew.

Fiction

# Blue House

*Claire Rudy Foster*

The house was blue when I found it. When I drive by now, my windows rolled up, breath humid on the glass, I see that the new owner has paid to redo the driveway and paint the house a fashionable shade of mustard. The window sashes, which were once the color of Vegas swimming pools, are a muddy red. I hate the new paint.

In my dreams, I am walking through this house, the blue house that is blue on the inside as well. It is like walking through levels of water, like walking out into the sea. I was at the ocean one summer, huddled in the stringy reeds that border the side-walk by the beach. I was eating a picnic of lentils, and the wind blew sand into my food so it gritted between my teeth. My memory is like that now, little grains catching me by surprise. My dreams are often clearer than that summer, or any summer. After the proper amount of time, the events of my life run together. They become blurred, as if by tears or too many drinks.

Night times are clearer for me, if only because I know the blue house so well. I have crossed its tilting floor, dream after dream. Its interior is unexceptional, big rooms with built-in cabinets and molding around the walls. There is an abandoned chandelier, also blue, hanging in the front parlor. The chandelier absorbs light now instead of giving it away. If I look at it too long, my dream will change. In its undusted facets, I once saw the contorted face of my least favorite high school teacher. She was pushing an old-fashioned lawnmower, and she wanted to know if I had finished my final paper. She said my verb agreement was the worst of any student and pushed the lawnmower over my foot, and the silver ribbons sliced me open, right down through my shoe. I woke up that time in a sweat, wishing I still talked to my old classmates. None of them had liked her either.

The house of my dreams has become an uncomfortable place. Before it was bought by somebody else, and painted its new yellowy colors, I was perfectly happy to sit outside in my car, watching it from the street. But now, as the house changes one afternoon at a time, I begin to feel itchy. I can't tear myself away, but what I see does not soothe me.

My car is not distinctive, so the neighbors haven't noticed when I come to sit here. No one asks me what I want. The house is unoccupied by its new owners—the only person who sees me is the man they hired to redo the roof. He works slowly in

the sun, carefully sticking one shingle on at a time.
His radio blares the top salsa hits. I usually bring
some book to look at while I sit in the driver's seat,
listening to Mexican radio from the roof. Summer
is coming, and my sweat sticks me to the cheap
upholstery. The book is always the same—or else
I can't tell them apart. I read the same page over
and over again. I like that when I look up, the
house is there, the same on its lot as it is in my head.
Sometimes I confuse it with myself, tip from side to
side, as if my face has suddenly opened into a porch,
my tongue a set of stairs. On days like this, when
my head becomes the blue house, I try to stay away
from people. I don't want to alarm them.

More confusing than this are the nights when I
can't sleep at all. As of today, it's been two weeks,
and the closest I've come to sleep is a quick fading
out of consciousness. Then my head has the dead
hush that I've only experienced in libraries. It's as
if all my thoughts are holding their breath at once,
sliding books off the shelves with the dry rasp of
dead leaves. But that's what paper is, isn't it? Dead
leaves, pieces of trees. My thumbs leave their sweaty
smears on the cheap paperback I've brought with
me today. The words are printed too small in cheap
ink, and I can't concentrate on them. The radio on
the roof squawks, *"Que gigante! El Monster Truck!"*
My head keeps bobbing forward on my neck. I am

so tired that my eyes are crossing. It's after eight o'clock, past quitting time if you work twelve-hour days. The man on the roof flicks off his stereo and lays down his nail gun.

I blink, and when I open my eyes I am out of my car and standing in the grass on the front lawn of the house-that-once-was-blue. Because nobody lives inside it yet, the grass is still uncut and peppered with dandelion clocks. The long stems tickle my calves. The very longest ones touch the hem of my dress. I look up, tilting my head back. I can feel my ears opening, flapping like loose solar panels.

The sky is turning half-gray, signaling evening in my town. The trees are too high to see the sunset. It's coming up on the summer solstice, the longest day of the year and the shortest night. That's some consolation, knowing that even if I can't sleep, I won't be alone in the dark for very long. Time will pull me toward sunrise. Then I can walk around and drink coffee like the normal people who spend their nights with their eyes racing back and forth behind their eyelids.

There is a very long ladder leaning against the house so that the man can come down from the roof at the end of the day. He climbs down slowly, with the dignity of the Man in the Moon. On nights when the moon is out, it's harder to sleep than usual—its light is too white, too persistent. I prefer

the sun, which forces me to shut my eyes. My naked
toes are dug into the grass, and my head is sagging,
back and forth, changing slowly into a house-shaped
box. My hands wave at my side, limp and soft as a
pair of discarded shoes.

"Hey, girl, you okay?" he calls to me. If I wanted to
I could say something that would make him climb
right back up again. I feel old and terrifying. Has he
ever seen a girl with a house for a head? Has he ever
heard her speak? I bend down quickly and run my
useless fingers through the grass by my bare feet.

"I lost my keys," I mumble around my thickening
tongue. The light is going now, creeping back behind
the West Hills where the houses are stacked like so
many expensive plates. On the other side of those
hills are suburbs, miles and miles of boring little
houses arranged around strip malls and supermarkets—a whole state full of suburbs, where people like
the man on the roof live their undistinguished lives.

I curl my hands around a clot of grass and thick sod.
The house's new owners will probably import a new
lawn from the turf farms. They will want a whole new
start.

"No, I found them." I stand up again, and even
though my hands are empty, the man nods and
climbs all the way to the ground. His nail gun is
stuck in his belt, and he takes his hat off to swipe
at his face with his forearm. He looks away from

me, leaning down to turn on the spigot on the side of the house. I get back in the car and drive to my favorite place to drink.

It's a small bar, only five minutes from the blue house. I pass the single stoplight, careful to look for bicyclists. My head is lolling, too heavy for my

neck. I am afraid of hitting someone and smashing my face like a pumpkin against the steering wheel. There is a parking spot right outside the bar. I pull the car up to the curb and smooth my hair behind my ears. I slip on my shoes and wiggle my toes inside them. I do not want to stumble on my way in because then they will not serve me liquor. It is the law in this state.

I had a dream once that I was lying in the blue house. The floor was strangely warm under my back, as if the boards were breathing. The house filled with water, higher and higher, past the depth of most swimming pools. I drifted up the stairs, in and out of the three bedrooms on the second floor. At the end of my dream, my face was pressed into the attic ceiling. I woke up gasping. A pipe had burst in the ceiling above my apartment and my sheets were soaked with someone else's bathwater. Ordering my first drink, I have the same sensation.

The man on the barstool next to me is redheaded, and the hairs on his arm make a thick, golden carpet. I can smell his sweat. The redheaded man smiles at me, and I smile back.

"What are you drinking, *water*?" He nods at my glass. Is he flirting? My stomach sprouts an extra chamber, a cellar-shaped room, and begins to fill with dusty jars of preserved summer fruit.

"Vodka," I say. That's what I like to drink the most. I like two fingers of very cold vodka in a glass, with no ice. It looks like water but feels thick and unctuous against my throat, like the way water might be on another planet. I sip from my glass. He's drinking beer, probably the cheap two-dollar special.

"Wow," he says. He has a little pattern above his wrist, like a line of scallops tracking across his skin. I stare at it, trying to decide if it's a tattoo. The drinking has shrunk my head back down to normal size, but my eyes are still tracking back and forth. It's hard for them to grip the world.

I touch his wrist, a little too hard, and rub the patterned line. It leaves a black mark on my finger.

"What is that?" I ask.

He looks down at his arm, as if just remembering that it belongs to him. "My bike broke today."

I stare at him. He makes no sense.

"It's the edge of my rear-wheel cog. See?" He traces the scallops—*swoop swoop*—with his finger. "It's a grease print."

"I thought it was a tattoo," I say. I drink a little bit more and then somebody puts a loud song on the jukebox. He leans close to me, and his breath smells like beer and dry leaves.

"I hate this song," he says into my ear. My head tips toward him accidentally—is it the drink? I can feel my cheeks starting to color up.

The first time I saw the blue house, however many years ago I lived in its neighborhood, it was July. The lingering humidity gave a shimmer to the air. I remember walking by the blue house and it seemed to float above its patchy lawn, each piece of it painted a different, brilliant shade—blue like on a

stripper's eyelids, or like toothpaste, or the color of
a vein, pulsing in your arm. It took me by surprise.
I stood there watching it. I couldn't decide if it was
real or not, so I threw a handful of change at the
porch. I went home thinking about the way the
coins clattered on the wood. That night I dreamed
my first dream in the blue house, and I haven't left it
since. It fills my whole head now, awake or asleep. I
finish my vodka and swish it between my teeth, the
way mouthwash commercials tell you to do.

"Let's go somewhere else," I say to him, and
although he is a stranger and we have hardly said a
dozen words to each other, he hops off his barstool
to come with me. He is much taller than I am, but
much thinner, so I am not afraid of him. I put a
twenty on the bar, and we walk out into the hot
June night.

"Walking?" he asks, and I nod. The liquor is making me feel loose and happy, and I have the feeling
that I might actually sleep tonight. Not sleeping is
hard on my bones. It makes me feel brittle and thin,
as if my insides have become a tangle of driftwood. I
forgot to pay all my bills this month, so my phone is
turned off and my landlord has been leaving *Where
is the rent?* notes on my door. It makes me sway on
my ankles, this strange freedom. Without my bills
I have nothing holding me. I could just stumble
through life, sleeping on sofas in other people's

houses, going through the rooms of my blue house one night at a time.

He unlocks his bicycle from the rack next to my car. I pretend that my car isn't my car so he won't ask me for a ride. We walk back through the neighborhood toward the street where I've already spent my whole day. It's very dark now, purple almost, and quiet. The roof is half done. The shingles look silver in the light of the rising moon. I like moonlight because it obscures things that are obvious. Even a familiar face's deep pits—the eyeholes, the shape of the skull—disappear in the moonlight. It turns things that are known into strangers.

The redheaded man from the bar pushes his bike carefully beside him on the grass. The sidewalks in this neighborhood are very uneven, due to the trees pushing up the concrete. I know the way so well that I don't lose my footing. He trips a few times, swears, laughs. My head has moved a few inches over my right shoulder. My neck is furry with new grass, and as I walk it tickles my skin. I shiver, though I'm not cold.

I think he assumes we're going to my apartment. Men think like that. If he were to ask me for my phone number, I'd give it to him—it's out of service anyway. It occurs to me that I don't know his name, and in the barely-there light I think he could be anyone. I dreamed that I was in the parlor of the blue house, looking out the window. There was a sea of people pushing past me, all faceless, as if they'd put skin-colored nylons over their faces. In movies, bank robbers do this so they will be anonymous. The redheaded man could be a bank robber, if he didn't look so trustworthy.

We stand on the lawn of the house in my dreams, and he squints at it. It's possible to see, even from the sidewalk, that the place is completely empty. The sugar maple in the yard is untrimmed, and its dropped leaves litter the sidewalk. I take the redheaded man by the elbow and pull him toward the porch.

"You need to help me with the door," I say.

"Are you sure you live here?" he asks.

"Yes, I'm sure." I take his bike from him and drop it on the grass. Nobody will steal it. This is a safe place.

He follows me up the four stairs, now painted that muddy red to match the window sashes. We can see inside the big front window: the bare floors and swept-out fireplace. It is obvious that nobody lives here, but that doesn't make me nervous. In my dream, I am always the only real person in the house anyway. I would be afraid if, in my sleep, I met somebody else walking through my hallways, tapping on the walls, looking for me.

He knocks on the door, stupidly, and waits as if he expects an answer.

"Nobody home," he says and looks at me. "You don't live here."

"I live here sometimes," I say. I don't believe in lying.

"Do you have a key?" he asks, and I can tell he's on the verge of leaving. He is getting that angry heat around him that people get when they think you've made fools of them.

"No," I say. "The door is stuck." I look at his backpack, the heavy thing he brought with him from the bar. "Don't you have your bike tools with you? We could jimmy the lock."

"I'm not going in there." The redheaded man goes back down the stairs. The minute his shoes touch the lawn, my eyes start to go dim, as if I am in a car with the low beams on, driving through the darkness toward sleep. He says, "This is too freaky."

He picks up his bike. He has a note of hesitation in his voice, and I know that if I called him to me, he'd come back, hopeful, willing to believe whatever I told him. But my tongue is thickening in my throat again, and I think of the rooms that wait for me, just on the other side of the door. I am so, so close. Two weeks without sleep is such a long time.

"Goodnight," I call to the redheaded man. He pedals fast, one white ankle flashing back at me under his rolled-up pant leg. In a moment he is gone. He took his smudged wrist with him. I would have liked to kiss that smudge.

Then I put my hand on the doorknob and, as if I am already dreaming, it turns, soft as butter, against my palm. The porch seems to sag under my feet in a sigh. I kick my shoes off toward the lawn. I hear them land in soft pats in the high grass.

I cross over into the house that was once blue, and in the moon's half light, it changes back to the way I remember it, the way it looked that first time in summer. The mustard paint and muddy trim fade to gray. My eyelids droop. I could be drowning. I could be walking into the sea. The first boy I really loved, I watched him drown many summers ago. I was no more than six, in my first two-piece swim-suit. Neither of us knew what the undertow was. I was furious that I wasn't allowed to go in after him, furious at the lifeguard for keeping me on the shore. Some nights I dream this boy back into life, and sometimes I find him floating facedown in the kitchen sink. I am careful as I shuffle barefoot across the floor of the blue house. I reach out and feel with my toes, so if I find him here I will be able to step back.

The light sockets are stripped. Their twin wires, capped with black plugs, are twisted like fishing worms. I brush them with my fingers. I imagine them exploding with those tiny electric stars, setting the house alight, licking my hair to a flame. I find the stairs exactly where my dreams have told me they would be, and I climb them. My body shifts, rolling like a ship. I am so tired that I am nearly blind. I push myself forward into my bank of memories.

Each room is empty. One bedroom has the traces of painter's tape around the doorway. Otherwise there is nothing. I expected to find a bed here, the covers neatly turned down, sheets cool and inviting. Instead I am greeted by crickets, which I can hear even through the painted-shut windows, and the rasp of my own acid breath in my teeth. I put my hand on the wall. My knees buckle under me, my sleeplessness bearing down on my shoulders.

The toilet in the upstairs bathroom is gone. The new owners must be installing a different one. The mirror, even, is taken down. There is a pale brown square over the sink, and I stare into it out of habit. I push my hair behind my ears. I close my eyes and rest my forehead against the place where my reflection should be. The wall is disconcertingly cool on my face. My ears begin to ring, and for a moment I am sure that I will lose consciousness. My mind slips away from me, shining like a dropped knife.

The bathtub—too small, a clawfoot built for tiny people from a long-gone century—holds me. I turn both knobs all the way on with my toes, but they only dribble rusty water. I had hoped to flood the house. Its walls are already blackened with sleep. I close my eyes and listen to my lungs. My breath makes the sound of waves, turning over and over on a rocky beach.

I sleep. For the first time, I do not dream. If there is a house in my head tonight, it is black and empty the way astronauts tell us space is empty.

"Girl. Girl. You okay?" It's the man on the roof.

His hand is on my shoulder, and I resent it. I am curled deep in my black sleep, waiting for the dream that is not going to come. I open my eyes just a slit. A huge brown face floats over me, a flesh balloon. My head feels heavy, still, but it is no longer a house. It has subsided, from walls and doors and windowpanes, to a simple hangover. The old taste of vodka cleaves to the inside of my nose.

"Girl?"

He has his radio in his free hand as he shakes my shoulder. For only a moment, I think he has come down from the shingles to tell me that the blue house is mine. I think I have awakened at last holding the polished stone of that lost summer. My eyes begin to sting with tears.

"I am fine," I slur. His hand is weighing me down. I can feel each of his five logical fingers pushing into my flesh, cool as coins. He bears down on me with his handful of words. It is as if he has rolled something back, some layer of skin or wood, and found me crouching in the splinters. If I were to close my eyes to him—plunge back toward my house of dreams—even then, the blackness would not hide me from the questions, the concern. I am being pulled up to the surface again, like a fish, taken from the deeps and pressures of the only place I know.

# The Graves of the Nephilim

*Alex Davis*

The Nephilim were on the earth in those days—and also
afterwards—when the sons of God went in to the daughters
of humans, who bore children to them.

—Genesis 6:4

Forgive me if my heart cringes with those who die,
Forgive me, friend, when even in thought I cannot be brave
Who think of your clear face agonized under tons of sky
Hourly growing more haggard from the weight of the grave.

—Oscar Williams, "Variations on a Theme"

Even before I knew why she believed her eyes
were gray, I hated my mother's rambling. She had
rambled enough, even before her senility, to wrangle
me into a narrow guilt; I spent two days a week
in her sunny, egg-yolk yellow room with the TV
on mute and orbited by a constellation of nurses
who seemed numb to the smell, the wrinkles, the
melanoma.

"You know how I value my mind, Jonathan. You
know that I'm passionate about"—I can still hear
the sizzle of her lips around the final word—"reason."

How many times had she made me promise in sarcasm, surrender, frustration, dismissal, boredom, betrayal—even occasionally in sincerity—never to abandon her, or not her, rather, but her head?

"You know I always love seeing you. But the telephone will be fine. I only want you to talk with me. Help me keep my mind. Promise you will help me keep it."

Maybe I hated the promises—the single vow spawned a thousand times. Maybe they were the invisible mites of what had become an intolerable itch, sheets left unwashed too long, now incited by her chattering into a bed of fleas. I hated how her words felt in my head. Their scattered shells milled around my nose and ears, always clicking, but always without a bite.

Yet I always returned, self-condemned. I wanted to be reasonable. I wanted to act like an adult—to feel the calm return of responsibility. But as her incoherence escalated with each visit, my integrity descended from dutiful desire to the drone of habit. I was miserable; she was oblivious. I was miserable because she was oblivious—to everything, but especially my misery. I chafed under two measly visits a week; I had been ready to quit long ago. But she had made me promise to help her keep her mind.

She might as well have made me promise to drink the red dribble that ran down her chin as

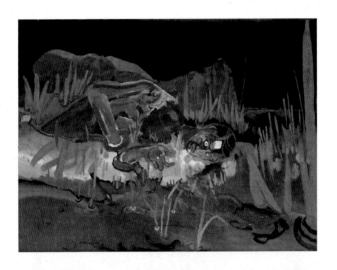

she babbled after being spoon-fed her medicated raspberry Jell-O. Listening to the woman's mindless words drilled a hole through the center of my eyes, back through time and space, and I began to despair that, in all of history, any words had ever really managed to speak order into life.

For my visit on the sixteenth of November, I wore my last clean shirt, an old red-and-black checkered flannel. It was the kind my father had worn in the years before he died.

Mother sat up smiling as I walked into the room, propping herself up on a few pillows. There was a strength about her movements that seemed completely misplaced. Her eyes—always that stormy gray—were clear.

"Terry." She greeted me with my father's name.

"Dad's dead, Mom."

"Terry, I need to speak with you before Jonathan arrives." She beckoned me to come near. "I may be dying."

I told her she was fine.

"Please, Terry. I may be dying. You need to know the truth."

"The truth about what?"

"I never told you everything."

"Everything about what?"

She slumped back down. Her eyes clouded, though they were still clearer than usual, and she mumbled, "The truth."

I asked her again, "About what?"

"Terry?" She was beginning to lose the thread of thought. "Terry, I need your help."

Generally speaking, I have a guilty conscience, but to this day I feel fine about what I said next. I lowered my voice. I rounded the edges of the words, smoothed them into the faded southern accent my father had never lost. "Quickly, Natalie. Tell me what's bothering you. Before Jonathan arrives."

She sat up again—suddenly strong and alert once more. "I never told you everything. Will you forgive me?"

"I forgive you, love. Tell me what's bothering you."

"I never told you," she whispered, and her body suddenly shook. "I was afraid. I was afraid of what you'd think. They saw me on the beach that day. They were digging with their spears." She began making a strange sound. "*Sshhhooof! Sshhooof!*" It was a guttural noise—the timbre too deep, the inhalation too strong for her frail chest to account for. "They were burying their dead. I know it. I saw what happened. I was there. I knew them already. Terry, I knew them."

I glanced over my shoulders. We were alone. "You mean the Nephilim." I spoke the name softly, distinctly. I had never dared use it in her presence.

Her eyes were at once wet and afire. "Yes!" Silence cradled the affirmation. She rocked a little in her bed. "You always believed me. You always did. I told you what they were like. I told you how I saw them. I never told you what happened, though, why everyone died. Forgive me."

"I forgive you."

Everyone in my family would have known what she meant—or rather, when she meant. My mother was a lady who had enjoyed several small, distinct strands of fame. She had written three textbooks on anthropology. She had never lost the pie-baking contest at the Whatcom County fair. She was carded at the bar until she was forty—each time an honest mistake. But, in its way the most famous of all, she had been part of an event she refused to discuss. In 1937, near her father's archaeological dig along the southwest coast of the Dead Sea, her family and a handful of other scholars had been massacred. The best speculations blamed Nazi allies, perhaps even followers of Husseini. Mother would say nothing. It was, to my knowledge, an event she never spoke about, even to my father. All we knew had come through the one word, *Nephilim*, mumbled in nightmares. The rest was family rumor and myth-making.

People who knew about her miraculous survival often made the mistake of asking her how she had managed it. Her answer was always polite, always obscure, always the same. "Why do any of us survive?" she would say with a tight smile. "That is a question for God."

My mother never held to a creed. She observed no religious traditions. But in her evasion she always made that unique reference to the divine. It puzzled everyone. That was all right. She was a puzzling lady in many ways.

But her silence was not all right any longer—not with me. The puzzle of her mind had slid to the edge of the table and fallen; the pieces were scattered across the floor. The pieces mocked her memory. They mocked my own. They formed another festering thing trapped under my skin. I needed to hear more; to the point of physical agitation, I needed my mother to share her secret self. Whether she wanted to or not, whether she was crazy or not, I did not care.

At that moment, my heart's flurry made me recall what my doctor had said weeks before about the risk my weight posed. I felt afraid, not of dying, but of dying before I heard her secret. In the face of her lucidity, I felt like a new father holding a baby born without bones—any movement might tear it apart at a dozen nascent points.

I asked her what she meant, what had happened. She opened her mouth.

My cell phone rang, the jingle from *Bonanza*. Mother's eyes instantly clouded. The tune ripped her mind from one decade to another. The driven woman—her firm lips, her auburn hair, her probing eyes—started nagging me through the dry ghost she had become.

"Turn off the television, Jonathan. You should be studying. You know what I think about those Westerns."

I cannot say if I have ever experienced loss more poignantly. The moment was lost. The thread of truth, the clarity in her eyes, the young woman with the brilliant mind—not to mention the stalwart boy she intended to raise—were all lost, now as spectral and faded as the story of the Nephilim.

I could smell yellow in the air, yellow hiding under the bed, yellow as it ate away at teeth and skin in every room around me. I smelled it—the faintest hint of ammonia, the pungent sweetness of frail bodies stewing in pent-up sweat—on everything. It was the smell of loss.

Mother, oblivious once more, rambled on. But I visited her every day for a month. I wore the same flannel shirt and a tweed cap. I brought everything of my father's I could find. Nothing worked. Every trigger failed. Her mind drifted through time. She cycled through precious memories, changing them to tragedy by her very babbling. She was unaware of how effectively it all tormented me. Words failed. Looks failed. The feel of my promises to her began to take on a yellow film. "Help me keep my mind. Promise me. Help me keep it."

I had to get away.

For two weeks I stopped visiting my mother. But in those two weeks, she never left my mind. I was suddenly obsessed with her secret and flew to the two places I thought might give me answers. I went to Jerusalem first, and from there I traveled down to Dimona and then due east to the site where my grandparents and uncles had been killed—where they were all cut down with blades, where my mother should have died, where perhaps a part of her did. Then I went to England, where an obscure shop-front museum in Durham housed the collection of my grandfather's records. Most of his papers were stained with blood.

In the public records I discovered little more than speculation. Perhaps some sort of Nazi caravan had taken an interest in their camp on that November morning; perhaps the boys had been cast to sea and that is why their bodies were never found; perhaps it had been a bayonet that cut across the back of my grandmother's neck as she ran toward the beach; perhaps my mother had been hiding in the dig before the massacre began—which was exactly where they found her, catatonic under a tarp.

I didn't need the records to tell me what happened; I merely needed a clue to my mother's mind. The documents on hand were full of academic notes, site logs, ledgers, special documents from regional authorities, the history of the Nephilim, the legends—both occult and sacred—and schematics of future digging plans. I quickly discarded all of these as irrelevant. Instead, I pored over a gilded journal the size of my hands; it had been my grandfather's. In it, among colorful accounts of his children's adventures, I found an entry that would send me home.

*Natalie will not be torn from the beach. She explores it even against our threats of discipline. I know she feels its poetry. I can see the weight growing in her eyes. She feels the history, the immensity, the mystery. What pleasure it brings my heart! Yesterday, after disobeying yet again and being found in the dig, Ailene sent me off to scold her. I knew, as I came into view of the beach and saw her shadow against the water, that my worst scolding would be a laugh. I would take her in my arms, and we would feel each other laugh. She knows my heart. My secret heart. She listens. I am sure that is why she disobeys. She wants to hear the water. She wants to hear the sand as it scatters. My disobedient girl listens. She knows their secrets are hiding here, curled somewhere in the sand. She knows their ghosts are near, speaking for those who will listen.*

As soon as I arrived back in Portland, I picked Mother up. I did not say a word during the two-hour drive to the coast. The town of Neskowin hides there, between tourist spots and a series of sea stacks, all in the cowls of low-blown clouds. I have never seen the sun in Neskowin, but I have seen many rocks, black and lonely, strewn along the wild beaches. I took her there on instinct; something in me had superimposed the memory of those black stones over my mother's eyes.

*Something in me had superimposed the memory of those black stones over my mother's eyes.*

I know a back road to a restricted stretch of beach called Beard's Hollow. It is an abandoned road that is flooded all year round. As we drove along its narrow canal, under a tunnel-row of Oregon ash, the staunch aroma of brine filled the air. Mother bobbed her head out the window and started popping between memories: Her honeymoon. Dad wearing his sand-crusted shoes to bed. Our infamous family reunion, broken up by rangers when Mom refused one of them a cut of steak. The day she awed her children with a sand castle walled completely with gleaming white shells.

I listened to the froth of words. Her rambles felt right. In the dark passage of trees, in the smell of salt and decay, I was alive to her ringing voice. It became the center of every other sensation carrying on the brisk Pacific air.

When we had pulled onto the beach, I put on the flannel shirt. I took her hand. We walked out toward the dark reflections of sky on water and those desultory stones lying before the ocean. The stones gleamed. They created the darkest reflections of all.

"Natalie," I said softly, "it feels as though we're there, doesn't it? On their beach?"

Mother gave a faint smile. "Whose beach?"

"Theirs."

"Oh, theirs," she said, uncertain. "It does?"

Gulping down a thrill of despair, I began offering leading questions, prods, nudges, hints—anything to elicit something about the Nephilim. In my mind, we were going to walk until one of us died or I got the story. But after fifty yards the old woman stopped, teetering. "I'm tired, Jonathan. Let's go back to the car."

My hands twitched with a desire to throw her into the ocean—an impulse of love, I think. But I only sighed. For some reason that sound—the sound of my own loss of breath, of my own helplessness—led me to pick up a shell and draw it to my ear. It was too small. I could hear nothing.

"That's how I found them."

There was nothing subtle about my reaction: I faced her instantly—and her eyes were suddenly passages into the past. She watched me closely but, at the same time, she did not seem to be watching me at all.

"I would walk about every day, staring at the sand. I searched everywhere. I could feel them. But they were hidden. They were hidden too well. Then I did what a child might do. I began skipping stones, out of instinct only the black ones. And then I found one buried under the stones. A shell in its tiny cairn."

"A shell?" I could feel the anticlimax in my bones. "There are no shells there, Mom. It's the Dead Sea."

She started off again, away from the car, toward the gulls that dawdled on the water's rim. The birds reminded me of old men at a funeral that were confused about when to put their jackets on. Mother plodded onward too, with a dawdle of her own. She kept between the waves, and I, put to relief against the sea stacks. For an instant I felt as though I was moving and that she remained fixed in the sand; I circled her craggy form, and only next to my motion could she pretend to move.

After a time she spoke. Her words sounded easy, potent: "My father dug up the beach systematically. He found no bones. I believed in him, though. I believed if he knew the burial grounds to be there, they were there. So I made my own search. I scoured for the only bones I could imagine. I explored that beach, digging cairn by cairn, gathering shell by shell. And Terry," she turned to me with eyes that glistened, "I broke a shell one day. And then another and another. Somehow I knew that brought them, silent, tremendous against the empty sky, sheaving the earth with their spears— *Sshhhhooof! Sshhhooof!*—mumbling strange things against the kings of Jerusalem."

I could feel my shoulders hunching. My fists were clenched. "The bones," I said, exhaling. "What happened?"

Her small white tennis shoes crunched over a pile of brittle seaweed. "They came with new shells to plant, not indigenous, no. Then they summoned waves. The waters rose and rushed in. The sand above the graves bubbled, and it grew bright hot, white, and red. And then it all went gray—a gray that burned into my eyes. It left a dead spot when I looked away." She wobbled and reached for my arm with a vein-riddled hand. "Their silhouettes…I still see them when I'm about to sleep."

She closed her eyes and frowned faintly, holding my arm. We continued forward, slow as the fog on the forested hills to the east.

We came upon some seagulls. Distracted by a string of disintegrating flesh, they suddenly felt our approach and burst into the air. Mother's eyes opened again.

"I found more, always the same, cast tall against the sea, the spears, the glow, the blind spot where the sand faded. They left only the shells, like coals, like dreams—nothing but mouths that told only one story, and even then, nothing but its final line." Mother inhaled violently, as though in pain. The waves seemed far closer than they were. "Then one day they saw me. They all saw me. They knew what I had done. And I remembered the stories. I remembered what they wanted with the daughters of Eve. But I couldn't get away." Her desiccated lips twitched toward a bitter upturn. "It was just then that the rest were murdered. I always thought the timing unbelievably odd."

"But was it the Mufti? The Germans? How did you know to hide?" Desperate for a confession of more than hints, I stabbed with my sharpest knife. "How…how did you survive?"

At those words, her head snapped up, and her gray eyes fled. I knew I had lost. "Who knows?" she said. And then, as though partners with her in an ancient rite, I mouthed the words that came next, even as she said them, "That is a question for God."

I took her hand. It was time to go. I knew she would be gone for a good while. And even if not, I was spent. We walked back toward the car.

Had she given away her secret somewhere in those scattered words? How much still lay hidden? Mother began babbling comfortably about diapers and breadcrumbs. But before we turned from the hard rim near the water to cross the soft row of sand where the car waited, I spotted a wide shell bigger than my hands. Mother saw it too. She gasped.

"Oh, that is one of them! Take it, Terry! You will see. You will believe me."

I released her hand to pick up the shell, not indigenous, no doubt a bauble dropped by a tourist who had become preoccupied with other things.

When it came to my ear, I studied mother's face.

"It reminds me of when you were a boy," she said, closing her eyes with a smile. "It was on this very beach. You picked up a sand dollar and pretended it was a shell. You yelled that you heard giants sleeping under the sand." She laughed, a small crinkling sound. "Giants under the sand. Everyone winked over your head. But I have never been so delighted. Or haunted. I have never felt nearer to anyone."

Mother took my hand. Then she was still. The tremble in her body passed into me, and I suddenly felt as though I was an hourglass sifting fine-grained sand. Her smile was as subtle as the arc of the coastline, and her eyes were closed again. But were they clear? The shell's lips brushed the tip of my ear, and along with its thrum, I could hear manifold echoes unified in a din. There was the rush of the waves, the thud of my heart, the haunting *shoof* of shovels in the sand, and the drone of an old woman's voice circling, circling, but never quite touching, the graves of the Nephilim.

# Strands
*Aliya Whiteley*

Faye had everything she had pursued: a husband, a baby, a career of sorts. To tell the truth and admit that none of these things were what she'd thought they would be seemed shameful, although she supposed a lot of people felt that way. It was only that she had never considered herself to be the type that got what she claimed she wanted, only to moan about it afterwards.

Still, it grew, this bud of dissatisfaction, until she could feel it tapping its sturdy little shoots against her internal walls, and she knew it was only a matter of days before it found a way through her defenses.

As it turned out, it wasn't a matter of days. It was a matter of years.

Ellie was about to start school. Her uniform had been bought, name tags sewn into the jumpers and the skirts, and they were counting down on the calendar to the day with the big red ex. The sense of expectation ruined everything Faye tried to do. Her

yoga was fast and jerky, and her handmade cards
had jagged edges and a rushed look to them that she
couldn't correct.

Faye had bathed Ellie before reading her a *Just So*
story and putting her to bed—doing all the things
that were expected of her so that nobody could
suspect that she didn't actually enjoy spending time
with her daughter.

She was busy submerging her usual attack of guilt
for the evening in a soap opera when she heard the
back door open and close, then voices, and laughter.
Matt had come home late from work with a friend
in tow, and although that was unusual, she was too
tetchy to let new company please her. For a start, she
was already in her dressing gown.

"Faye? Is there any red wine?"

"Just what's in the rack," she called, then got up
from the sofa and wandered into the kitchen with
half a mind to be unpleasant.

Matt's friend stood with his back to the sink, his
hands stretched out along the counter. He appeared
old and tired. He looked up at her with evident
surprise. "Hello," he said.

Matt straightened from the wine rack with the
neck of a bottle of Merlot in his hand. He had
already removed his tie and undone the top button of his shirt; his jacket hung over the back of
the metallic counter stool. He kept fit during his

lunch hours, and every day he looked more as if he belonged in a glamorous life that was taking place somewhere else. "Phillip, this is my wife, Faye."

"Hello," Phillip said again, and she revised her first impression of him. He wasn't old, although he was undoubtedly older than she was. His graying hair was cut close to his head, revealing high temples and large ears, and although there were long, sloping lines on his face, his eyes and mouth were generous and energetic—the features of a boy who had not yet been taught to keep his emotions discreet.

Faye tightened the belt of her dressing gown over the bulge of her womb, a leftover from pregnancy that remained immune to exercise. It seemed obvious to her by the way he held his head that he liked her.

"I'll go and get changed," she said. "Have you eaten?"

"Ate out," said Matt. "I meant to phone but the battery ran out on the mobile again. Didn't I ask you to remind me to charge it?"

That was Matt in a nutshell. He could handle the liquidation of huge companies. Without blinking, he could lay off thousands of people at the behest of the accountancy firm he worked for. And yet, he was unable to realize that the objects he relied upon every day just needed a small amount of maintenance. His pen ran out or his car missed a service, and then

invariably he tried to put the blame on Faye, as if it was the duty of a wife to maintain his life for him while he worked on more important things.

"Please don't get dressed on my account," said Phillip. His voice had a tone of humor in it that made her smile back at him despite her resolution to be annoyed.

"All right," she said. "I won't." It came out, in the strangest way, like a challenge. Matt was battling with the corkscrew and didn't seem to notice.

"Grab the good glasses and take them through to the living room, will you? We're celebrating. Closed an account at work."

"Well done."

She turned her back on them and walked self-consciously through the hall to the dining room, where she took three of the blue Murano glasses from the display shelves. She cleaned off the dust using the hem of her dressing gown and walked back to the living room with her mind on how she must look to Phillip—like a tame housewife? Or maybe, hopefully, like a glamorous figure with her hair up from the nape of her neck and her silk dressing gown sweeping the floor. She decided to believe that he found her beautiful. Then she could act like a different woman because of it. A little pretense would be very welcome.

Phillip had taken the armchair by the recessed fireplace, and Matt was lying back on the sofa. Faye handed out the glasses and sat on the floor by Matt's legs, acutely aware of her bare feet, the soles facing Phillip as she stretched out her own legs and tucked her dressing gown under her knees.

Matt leaned over to Phillip and poured him a glass first, then Faye, then himself. The first sips passed in silence, as if they were connoisseurs rather than just ordinary people searching for something to say.

"Faye, how was your day today?" said Phillip.

"Fine," she said, shocked into giving a boring answer.

"Not long until Ellie starts school now," said Matt in a hearty tone. "Faye's dreading it."

"Actually," she said. "I'm quite looking forward to having some more time for myself."

"She'll be miserable at first. Still, she's got a little business, making greeting cards. It's going quite well, keeps her occupied."

"Yes," said Faye. "Are you married, Phillip?"

"I have been. Three times." He held his wine glass very lightly, his fingers moving up and down the long stem.

"Wow."

"Yes," he said, as if it was a puzzle to be solved, so she dared to ask about it.

"What went wrong?"

"Absolutely nothing," Phillip wrinkled his nose at her, and she saw the lines around his mouth intensify. Exactly how old was he? "I suppose I don't believe anything is forever."

"I keep telling Phillip he should have kids," said Matt. "Kids make you appreciate just what forever means."

"That's true," Faye said.

"You're not committed to anything unless you choose to be," Phillip replied, in a friendly tone, but she noticed how upright he sat, how he hadn't removed his jacket or loosened his tie. He hadn't fallen for the idea that he could relax in her presence because she was a wife. She was surprised to discover she liked him at least as much as he liked her. She wanted him to stay longer.

"You're sure I can't get you something to eat?"

"No, no," he said. "I should get going."

"You've only just got here!" said Matt, as she knew he would. He always tried to persuade guests to stay. "C'mon, let's finish the red, and I'll open a bottle of something special." That was his code for Cognac, and that meant hangovers tomorrow and the smell pervading the house, her breath. But it also meant Phillip would have to take the spare bed and she would make him breakfast in the morning. A little piece of him left behind in the house, on the sheets, in the crumbs on the fine china.

"Maybe another time," he said.

From the top of the stairs came a trembling voice. "Daddy?"

Faye felt such guilty relief that Ellie had called for Matt, not for her. It was a gift—to be alone with an interesting man, to stay free of motherhood for a few moments longer. She leaned forward so Matt could stand up, his abrupt movements filled with self-importance. He adored this part of parenthood: to be needed. "That's my cue."

"She probably just wants a kiss and a cuddle," Faye said.

"That's my specialty." He went out into the hall, and she heard him take the stairs at a faster pace. Then he spoke to Ellie in that special way he had. Faye could picture him picking Ellie up, the way she nuzzled into the crook of his neck. It gave her a moment of pleasure to know she had created Ellie. It was a rare emotion, one she only experienced when she imagined father and daughter together.

If only she could have worked full time. He was better at parenthood. It came naturally to him. Whenever she tried to explain how she didn't feel the same, he talked of help or counseling, getting her fixed so things could go on as they should.

"Actually," said Phillip, as he stood up. "Something did go wrong. With all three marriages. I've yet to find a woman who believes in freedom as much as I do. Do you think a woman wants a man to be tied to her forever whether that brings happiness or torment?"

"Yes," she said, liking the words he used, the big concepts of which he wasn't afraid. "Or, at least, men should be tied down and made as unhappy as possible, as often as possible."

She could tell she'd surprised him. "Why is that?"

"How else can a woman make a man appreciate what motherhood is like?"

Straight away, she regretted saying it. The wall had finally been breached, and here, in front of this stranger. There was nothing that could be said to cover it. She didn't know him well enough to turn it into a joke—*You know me, my funny sense of humor.*

He licked his bottom lip. "Not everybody has to be..."

"What?"

"You don't have to be here."

"Is that your philosophy? Forgive me for saying so, but I can see why your marriages didn't work."

"How so?"

She got to her feet too, and realized how close that brought her to him. Still, she held her ground. "Sometimes it seems that men never love the way women do."

"Is that a good thing or a bad thing?"

She heard snatches of a lullaby, Matt's deep, happy voice.

Then Phillip cleared his throat. "I have a convertible. A BMW. It's a warm night."

"Really?"

And he would go, and she would be left here worrying about what he thought of her, who he would tell about what she'd said. Would the words *bad mother* come out of that generous mouth? At the office, the next day, would she be relegated to the status of anecdote? It took her by surprise, this fierce longing to change the path of their meeting, to not be dismissed, to make him feel something real.

"Come out for a drive," he said.

She had been so busy packaging herself as an embarrassment that she didn't hear him at first.

"A drive," he said again.

"When?"

"Now."

"I should…"

"Now," he said. "Quick." And he held out his hand with an urgency in his face, as if the worst thing in the world would be for her not to take it, so she took it, and they left the room, through the hall, the kitchen, out the back door, past the swing set and the empty bird feeder, down the alley to where the bins huddled, and out to the driveway. There was his

BMW, silver, the roof down, parked behind their Megane.

Phillip was right. It was a warm night.

He opened the passenger door for her, and she got in, tucking her dressing gown over her legs. As he walked around the front to the driver's side, she looked around the street, between the evenly spaced streetlights to the paths of her neighbors' houses—the formality of those painted front doors, the hedges that had been trimmed into squares

and rectangles. When he started to reverse the car, the noise was so loud that she pictured everyone running to the windows to stare out.

Beside her, he handled the car as men do, like a master guiding a willful dog, and without asking, he reclined her seat with a button next to the handbrake so she could see up to the sky. There was only the haze of the lights of the city and the occasional star: it had to be so bright to make it through all this interference to reach her eyes. Her sense of home, the strands of her that reached back to Matt and Ellie, spilled out behind her like spider silk, loose, bending, not even close to being stretched thin.

"I know a place," said Phillip. "In the country. You'll be able to see the stars out there. It's where I go when I want to be able to think."

"About what?" she said, surprised to find her voice sounded light, casual.

He shrugged. His profile was less friendly than the full view of his face. His nose was a long straight line, regal, reminding her of a Roman coin. For the first time she suspected he might be capable of cruelty.

"I like to think about the path ahead."

"That sounds very calculating."

"I like to have a plan."

"But this couldn't be part of your plan," she said, meaning herself.

"No. This wasn't in the plan."

"Sometimes," she said, "when I make my cards, I picture the people who'll receive them, and what they'll be doing. Wedding days, births, condolences. Will they all be feeling what they're meant to be feeling?"

"Does it matter what other people think?"

She didn't reply. She thought that nothing else could matter and was surprised to learn he thought differently.

"I've made a mistake," she said. "Take me back, please."

But Phillip didn't turn the car around, and she didn't ask again. His lack of obedience made her excited and fearful. She wondered when reality would kick in.

Matt would have come back downstairs by now. She pictured him hunting around the house, in the way he did when he played hide and seek with Ellie: bending low, looking under beds and in the linen cupboard. A laugh spilled out of her. How cruel she was. How terrible, and free.

They hit the motorway and the long untroubled lanes took her farther away, the strands still strong, still spooling.

After a while the scenery began to change. The flat plains curved upwards into hills, then forests, the trees pressing close. The motorway became a dual carriageway, then a single track, and the speed of the car lessened until it felt as if they were moving no faster than she could wait. She was cold now in the convertible, but she didn't ask for the roof to be put back up. She didn't want to accept that something had changed; that she was not in the car to see the stars anymore.

"Nearly there," Phillip said.

"Where?"

"The place I know." The new edge of tension in his voice put her on alert. What did he think was going to happen? How ridiculous she was not to have really thought about the possibility that he just wanted sex. Not that she hadn't considered having sex with him, but if he thought that was the reason she got into the car, how belittling that would be.

Had Matt given up by now? Gone to sleep, assuming she'd be back in the morning and no words would need to be exchanged about this transgression? Or did he think she had been taken against her will, spirited away?

Sometimes Ellie had bad dreams and needed to hear the song about the sleepy elephant. Faye wasn't sure if Matt knew the words. She could see Ellie quite clearly at that moment. In bed, in that ridiculous position she always managed to end up in, her head against the bed rail, her feet on the wall, her pajama top crumpled up and her face a blank sheet of peace in the purple glow of her nightlight.

That was responsibility; that clear image of the child who doesn't realize what adults are capable of and holds her mother ransom with her innocence.

The desire to get home was suddenly strong. She fought it down.

Phillip drove into a town through the silent main street. Faye had a vague idea that hours had passed. They turned left and began to climb. Then there was a view of the sea, black as tar. A right turn and in front of her was a manor house, two porch lights revealing gray pillars and a closed front door between many windows. The car stopped and she got out, feeling the painful prickle of gravel on the soles of her bare feet. Phillip came to stand beside her. "They know me," he said. "I'll get a room."

She looked at him, and he touched her neck with one finger. There was something proprietary in the gesture that made her want to brush him away, turn to him, demand proper answers. She could have said, *What exactly do you think of me? What is it that you think is happening here? Explain this connection in one-syllable words, taking no longer than thirty seconds, so I can get to the bottom of this.*

But she said nothing, and he went to the door and rang the bell, one of the old ones that he had to pull out from the wall. It made no sound that she could hear.

While his back was turned, she tiptoed across the gravel, bare feet smarting, and took a set of semicircular stone steps down into an overgrown garden that stretched over the hill, leading down to the sea. She walked on, the path changing to wood chippings—easier on the feet—and she brushed past tall, leafy plants that she didn't recognize. The sense of being watched grew with each footstep—watched by animals, birds, by the sea itself. Yet she felt connected to the ground she walked upon and to the leaves she ran her hands across. She could hear the sea now, shushing her, assimilating her. For the first time since the birth of Ellie, she did not feel out of place.

Farther down, the path petered out in the face of a wall of dense bushes, and as she pressed into them, their wetness soaked her dressing gown, and their branches snagged the material. She undid her belt, slipped off the gown, and carried on in her short nightdress, letting the night air steal all her warmth away, take her heat and her emotions for its own.

Behind her, a voice—

"Faye!"

She crouched on an instinct, and then turned, moving her head until she had a view of the path back through the leaves. Phillip was there, at the bottom of the stone steps, his close-cropped hair silver in the moonlight. He stood still and tall, and it struck her how handsome she found him, but she did not move.

He waited, as if it was inevitable that she would come to him, and the longer he waited, the more she turned against him. A man was never going to provide an answer. Men, with their lives laid out in straight lines, like motorways, each emotion taken at a time, never overlapping, all in perfect order: daughter, job, house, wife, and always one part, the deepest part, free and clear. Men came with a fast lane, for themselves only, no baggage allowed.

How had she fallen for it?

Phillip looked over his shoulder, then out to the sea. He said something she couldn't hear, then called again: "Faye!" The garden trembled at his voice.

He walked away.

And then there was nobody left to escape. The strands of her life, spilling out from her in all directions, didn't tighten, didn't pull at her. They were slack, and somehow the garden had freed her of all emotion: guilt, fear, love, sucked down into the soil and locked away, deep in the earth, like a foretaste of death, so welcome.

Faye pulled her nightdress up over her head and threw it away. She walked farther into the bushes, heading for the sea.

# Schadenfreude

*Caren Coté*

For nearly two years it's been my habit to drive
to work in silence—I bought my car based on
the manufacturer's silent-ride claims. Except on
Wednesdays. One radio show is still capable of
inspiring the occasional laugh: Wednesday's *Those
Crazy Germans* segment. Last Wednesday, I heard a
word that changed my life. *Schadenfreude*: enjoyment
obtained from the troubles of others. Technically, it
didn't so much change as define my life. The second
half of my life.

"There's a word for it," I whispered, even though
I was alone in my car, waiting for the light to turn.
"It's validated."

I thought of the day last winter when I'd slipped
on a patch of ice in front of Safeway and broken my
ankle. Everyone in view laughed as though they
were watching a home video show. I sat there, the
ice melting into the back of my skirt and thighs,
crying and rubbing my ankle, until the store man-
ager came out and asked if I needed any help. I said
yes and made it an apology. His question had been
an accusation.

While the doctor put a cast on my ankle, I thought of those people who'd laughed and how they'd tell the story at work, at their dinner tables, at seedy bars, and get big laughs.

"Get a load of this," they'd say, their rotten front teeth and putrid lives temporarily forgotten, their slack expressions replaced by the joy of reliving the experience. "This woman, this funny-looking, middle-aged woman with bright orange curly hair— she looked like a leprechaun or something—was walking into the Safeway in high heels this morning, and she slips. Her arms go out, like she's trying to fly instead of fall or something. Her little purse breaks, and all the stuff falls out on the ice—you can hear a crack as she hits the ground! It was so trippy! She just sits there while people pocket her stuff and walk into the store!"

Then everyone would laugh, and someone would say, "What a great story! Let me buy you a drink."

When I got my cast, the doctor's assistant asked whom she could call to come pick me up. I couldn't tell her I had nobody to call, so I lied and said my family was on vacation and to please call me a cab. The next day I took another cab to get my car from Safeway's parking lot. At least then I had something to be thankful for: automatic transmissions.

When the doctor's assistant called to make the appointment to get my cast removed, she said to

have someone drive me in case my ankle was sore afterward. When I got to the office, she asked when my ride was coming back, and I blurted out that I'd driven myself. She frowned at me over the top of her glasses as though I were her disobedient daughter. Out came the truth: "I had to drive myself, okay? All my friends stopped knowing me after my son killed himself and my husband left."

She laughed.

A few moments later, she realized I wasn't joking and her ears turned red. She looked down at the papers on her desk and said to have a seat and the doctor would be right with me. Even though I could tell she was trying, she couldn't get the smile to completely leave her face.

I pulled into a parking space at work and sat in my car for a few minutes, thinking, rolling the word around in my mind. *Schadenfreude.* I said it aloud, to see how it felt. I kept saying it until I saw one of the security guards in my rearview mirror, walking across the parking lot toward me. I got out before he reached my car.

"Everything okay, Miss Stephens?" he asked when I passed by him.

"Yes, thanks. My favorite song was on the radio, so I stopped to listen to it."

He'd been close enough to my car to know that was a lie. As I walked inside, he stood there and laughed.

I whirled to face him and demanded that he tell me why it was so funny—in my mind, of course. I couldn't do a thing like that. I just said, "Schadenfreude," and kept walking.

After work, I stopped at a tavern that had been a farmhouse about a hundred years ago—my intention to drink many mason jars of raspberry beer and walk the last three blocks home carrying my shoes. I wanted to celebrate my new word in the same way I'd celebrated my husband's first promotion about a hundred years ago.

In the yard behind the whitewashed Queen Anne–style building, where generations of kids had climbed trees, had their first kisses, and recited wedding vows, sat a dozen picnic tables for people to sit in the shade or in the sun—or in the rain, I suppose—drinking and hanging out with their friends. Most of the tables were full, but one had only three people, one man facing a couple. The other half of the table was empty, so I sat down there in the sun. I've read that this kind of thing is natural in Europe—strangers sharing a table—so it annoyed me when those three happy people clucked their tongues and slid an inch or two down their benches, as far away from me as they could get. My sitting on the far side of one of the benches, both legs over the short end with my back to them, didn't take anything away from them. They whispered for a while.

Soon enough they started to pretend I wasn't there and went back to talking and laughing in their normal voices. This allowed me to indulge in my favorite hobby: eavesdropping. Reading novels had been my favorite hobby, but since my life's been gone I prefer the unedited, carelessly thrown-about words of real people to the way authors write. When I eavesdrop everyone sounds less educated than I am, but in novels it's all perfect. Now I read newspapers and nonfiction books. I can read those books and for a little while I live in Paris or Bangladesh, I'm a politician or an anthropologist.

The trio told each other the jokes from the latest teenage sex movie. Obviously they'd all seen the movie, but they laughed at every bit of its retelling. One of the men possessed impeccable comic timing—better than the actors in the movie—so I wanted to see his face, to know more about what kind of person he was. He sat across from the couple, on the bench opposite me, and as I stood up

I took a good look at him. He had a wild shock of dark red curly hair and at least a million freckles. I found him heartbreakingly handsome. I looked too long, and the other man asked, "Are you going to introduce us to your stalker?" All three roared with laughter.

I went back inside and wandered from conversation to conversation, drinking my second mason jar of beer. I smiled and moved on after making eye contact; everyone smiled back and returned to their conversations. They believed what I wanted them to—that I was looking for someone. Someone in particular.

Halfway through my third jar of beer, the handsome comedian appeared next to me. He made eye contact and smiled, and when I smiled back he didn't move on.

"Hi, I'm Robert."

"Hi." I nodded. "I'm your stalker."

He laughed a little too loudly and moved one step closer to me. I'd hardly seen a man so handsome who didn't dwarf me.

"Listen, I'm sorry about that. He had enough to drink long before you sat down. He shouldn't have said that."

"Okay."

"Can I get you another beer?"

He was waiting for me to tell him my name, so I said, "Colleen. Colleen Schadenfreude. You can get me another beer."

"Colleen, nice to meet you." We walked toward the bar. "That's an unusual last name. Is it German?"

"Yes. I'm German on my dad's side and Irish on my mum's." I laughed and watched Robert wonder about me. In reality, I was half Irish, half French, and half drunk.

We ordered fresh beers, and he asked if I'd rather sit there or outside. I pointed to two empty stools

near the end of the bar, and he said, "Cool." We had taken three steps toward the stools when I experienced what my new word felt like from the other side.

As we walked by a statuesque woman with long blond hair, she turned to leave the bar and hit Robert in the face with her full, quart-sized mason jar. Blood squirted from his nose onto the blonde, a single drop landing in her beer. It twisted and stretched through the accommodating liquid, and then Robert fell to the floor like a wet mop. My stomach churned, and my mouth tasted like recently unearthed coins. The blonde shrieked—a self-conscious sound, as though she made it to please her audience more than to express genuine emotion. She gave the room a quick glance and then kicked Robert with the pointy toe of her boot. Quite the performance. I thought maybe he'd been knocked out by the mason jar, but when she kicked him, he began wailing and didn't stop.

I laughed.

Some people joined in; others looked disgusted. A few backed away averting their eyes, and others moved closer to stare. I knew I'd be ashamed later, but I couldn't stop laughing. When tears streamed down my cheeks and I was the only one still laughing and people had started to help Robert and the blond girl, I set my half-empty jar of beer on the bar. I took the straps of both sandals in my left hand and walked home. I probably could have driven after only two and a half jars of beer, but I could not stop laughing.

I was still laughing as I entered my building and climbed the stairs, but silence caught up with me the moment the flimsy white door closed on my dark, empty apartment.

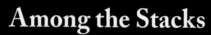

# Among the Stacks

*Andrew S. Fuller*

I was reshelving in the 900s when I came across the book. Seeing one corner of its unremarkable blue cover tilted slightly outward, I pressed it back into alignment, and it was then that I noticed the blank spine. This is not unusual with some older books, but—and I remember this distinctly now—the binding bore no Dewey decimal number or library sticker. Considering this and the absence of a library stamp on the page edges, my first thought was that someone had left a personal book in the stacks and I should take it to the lost and found.

Then I gasped, and nearly dropped the book, for the cover very plainly read *The Hanging Cities of Sorrow*. I shook what I assumed to be fatigue from my eyes; the title seemed hazily familiar in a way that created a faint yearning in my chest. The author, one K. E. Hurlefsonne, was unknown to me, and the lack of dust jacket gave me no marketing preview (a feature of modern books that I dislike). It was the only book I took home that night.

I planted myself in the reading chair immediately after arriving home and didn't move for four hours. Seven chapters unfolded before I realized that I'd missed dinner. I recall little plot now, but enough. It was the account of Rebecca Pulchridue, a shy maid-servant living on a nineteenth-century Yorkshire estate, helplessly traveling in time each night while she slept, to a different era in the far future, where she fought alongside her alien lover in the resistance against the cyborg dinosaur skeletons. I fell asleep near midnight, just as they were infiltrating the army breeding factory.

Hours later, I awoke and stretched, then resumed reading with chapter eight. My confusion deepened after a few paragraphs, as the terse first-person narrator Jack Crawling and his remarks about the insectile legs of the dame in his dingy office felt entirely out of place. Then I noticed the page heading. A misprint at the publisher seemed the likely explanation, for there was plainly written *Twilight of the Salamander* by Yid Xeston. I checked subsequent pages, disappointed and confused. They matched. Before the thought was fully formed in my mind,

a nervous chill tightened my skin. Though I knew I should not, I held my breath and flipped quickly back through the early chapters: more words in PI Jack's voice about the angle he was working on the wereamphibian sex ring case. The character Rebecca was nowhere to be found. I closed the book, squeezing the common blue cover with aching fingers and eyeing the new title.

I rose slowly, setting the book aside on the chair. I commenced a search of the living room, beginning with the few picture books on the coffee table. Breathing steadily, I looked through my bookshelves, then my bedroom. *The Hanging Cities of Sorrow* was not in my apartment. I stood for a moment, thinking I must have dreamed the Yorkshire maid and her futuristic adventure while dozing. I went to bed but could not sleep.

In the morning, the single blue book on the chair was *My Bones Cry Forth*. I refrained from hurling the volume across the room. After breakfast, I put the thing in my backpack without looking. On the bus ride, against my better judgment, I peeked into my bag and felt nausea when A. G. Jutman Kleenard's *Mastodon Lust* stared back at me. Resolved to lose the book in circulation, I dropped it in the outside return bin, but not before I glimpsed *Amaranthine Slaughter of Reveries*.

That afternoon I looked up all of the titles and authors from the unnerving tome, and am sure you can guess the results.

That was last spring. I have since checked out other books, but they sat on my bedroom floor in undisturbed stacks. I transferred to a different branch a few months ago, but it followed me. Of course I threw it away in the dumpster—a number of times. Still, it returns, appearing in every section of the library: fiction, nonfiction, reference, even periodicals and children's, and sometimes in my cart. I do not crack the spine of *The Wails of Bleeding Continents* or *Muted Voices of Ancient Ptor*. I bury my curiosity about *Blea's Undue Demise* or *Mr. Schlenkinback's Guide to Rancorous Relics*. I merely shelve it.

Sometimes in my dreams I am reading a book that I know does not exist, and the blue book appears in my waking life soon after with the very same title. Sometimes I wake at night with the urge to run downtown to the library and find the book.

I tried to open another book last week. But I sobbed uncontrollably instead.

Awake each night, I lie unmoving until the light comes.

# Powder Down
## *G. M. Hanson*

Jenner didn't look like an angel. He was haggard and dirty and often smelled like vomit. He wore his borrowed or stolen clothes a little too baggy, and he hadn't had his hair cut with anything other than a dull razor blade for the past several years. He was missing teeth, and painful sores riddled his body. No, Jenner didn't look like an angel at all. But that didn't change the fact that he was one.

The abandoned building in which Jenner sat was slated for demolition in two weeks. Once a prosperous department store, the edifice was now home to various unsavory characters. The couch upon which Jenner sat was a curious find. Dumped by the old railroad tracks, Jenner had called in a few favors from some buddies who helped him carry it the four blocks to this, its final resting place. Its floral pattern was a good match for the activities of this space because nothing hides small blood spots like sporadically placed roses.

This rundown room would be Jenner's temple—the temple in which miracles would be performed. Jenner had been doing the Lord's work for several years now but, like many angels, he was wholly unaware of his calling.

Jenner set up his altar on a makeshift coffee table made of cinder blocks and a slab of old kitchen countertop. He located his cooking utensils—a lighter and a spoon which earlier had been lodged between the sofa cushions, causing him some small amount of panic before he finally located them. He found a good-looking rig out by the trash can in the alley, and he cleaned it out a bit by plunging some water through the needle several times. He laid everything out before him, ready now to perform the ceremony.

"Jenner, my man!" bellowed a voice from behind him. Jenner turned to see a friend from the past.

"Garcia, buddy. What's up, mi amigo?" Jenner offered his hand.

"Not much, not much, my friend." Garcia took Jenner's hand and pulled him into a manly embrace. Garcia was happy to see Jenner. Really happy to see him.

"You're looking good, man," Jenner said. He welcomed the pleasant smell of Garcia's cologne, purifying the space with its scent.

"Been clean for four months," Garcia said. "Even got a job."

"Good for you. Really. Good for you, man."

Garcia lowered his head a bit. "I was hoping I'd find you here. Hoping you'd be willing to share a little shit with me." He motioned to the coffee table. "I got a little cash."

"Your money's no good here, my friend. Sit." Jenner moved his stained jacket off the couch, making room for Garcia. Garcia was a good man, and Jenner wanted to help the guy out.

"I've just been jonesing a lot lately, you know?" Garcia said. "Had a fight with the old lady. I just

need something to help me out a little. You know what I mean?"

"You got an old lady? How come I never knew that?" Jenner removed the belt from around his waist. He preferred women's belts because they cut off the circulation better than bulky men's belts. Besides, women's belts fell out of fashion so quickly, it was never hard to find one in neighborhood trash cans.

"She's a good woman, but she makes me fucking crazy, you know?"

Jenner said a little prayer as he consecrated the substance in front of him. *Please, God, let this be some good shit.* He moved his lighter under the spoon until its liquid bubbled. "Hold this," he said, handing the spoon to Garcia. He rummaged through his pockets for a cigarette filter, selecting one from the small amount he had collected in the past few hours. "There's a lot of good women out there. But that don't make them saints." He tore a small piece off the filter and placed it on the spoon.

Jenner filled his needle with the Lord's gift. He flicked the syringe until it was free of harmful air. He held the rig between his teeth and motioned for Garcia's arm. "She'll probably leave me for good after this," Garcia said. He rolled up the sleeve of his dress shirt and picked up the belt that lay between them. "You're a good man, Jensy. Sharing your dope. Even letting me go first."

Garcia wrapped the belt around his arm. Jenner ran his finger along Garcia's skin, searching for a thin tube just under the surface. Jenner's black fingernails moved slowly over the area until he could feel his target. He took the syringe out of his mouth and gently pierced Garcia's skin. "I'm only gonna give you a little, man. You've been off the shit for a while."

Garcia's lids dropped as the Lord's gift hit his brain. "No, I can take more," he began to protest, but that feeling, *that feeling*, consumed him, and as Jenner slowly removed the needle, Garcia slumped back against the couch, closing his eyes.

Jenner wiped off the needle with his shirt and took the belt from Garcia. As Jenner wrapped the belt around his own arm, he was grateful that it had healed enough to be used again. The spot on his foot—the spot he'd been using for several weeks now—had grown infected and inflamed, and digging around in his skin in search of a vein had become tiresome. With his arm healed, he was granted a straight shot.

Jenner watched as he allowed a small measure of his own blood into the syringe. *This is the blood of Christ*, he thought, *which will be given up for you*. He heard the faint ringing of a bell as he pushed on the plunger, filling his body with this, a most unholy communion.

A bird. A white bird. Standing on the banks of the lake. Wading slowly, the white plume feathers on its head moving up and then down. Jenner always sees the bird in his mind's eye. A white heron, he's sure of it. His mother was an ornithologist and the many hours he spent with her spying on winged creatures through the lenses of high-powered binoculars left him with a mound of useless knowledge surrounding the lives of birds.

The sound of a choir. Altar boys singing the praises of the Lord. He is crying. Jenner always sheds a tear. A lone tear filled with equal parts of pleasure and of sorrow because Jenner suffers in these moments of his greatest pleasure. Not unlike other angels, Jenner falsely believes he is forsaken.

The bird takes off. Flying above him, neck retracted, plumes lying down. It looks funny in the sky. Seems more natural at the lake's edge. Jenner can hear its wings flutter. Soon it's out of sight.

"Every man needs a good woman," Jenner continued when he returned to the world. He looked to Garcia who was still lying with his eyes closed. He was envious of Garcia. Having been clean meant Garcia was feeling so much more than Jenner.

Jenner lit a cigarette. With every drag, he could feel his front tooth move. It would only be days before it finally freed itself from his mouth. He touched it with his index finger. Wiggled it. Yep, only days.

Garcia held his hand out, requesting a drag off Jenner's cigarette. Jenner gave it to the man, and then lit another. The two men sat in smoky silence, listening to the distant chatter of other men just like them, across the littered room.

"She loves me anyway," Garcia said. "Even with all this." He moved his hand around in a circle. "Even with all this shit, all I've done to her, she still loves me, man. What the fuck am I supposed to do with that?"

"I don't know, mi amigo. Never really had me that kind of woman." Jenner took a long drag on his cigarette.

"What about that hot little number you used to get with every now and again?" Garcia asked.

"You talking about Sugar Tits? Thin little blond gal?"

"Yeah. Whatever happened to her?"

"Don't know. She just stopped coming around." Jenner stubbed out his cigarette on the altar table. The truth was, he had an idea of why she stopped coming around. Once, the two of them were in a real bad way, no money, no junk. Found some sleazy white guy on the west side who was willing to score them a little to hold them over, but "someone's gonna suck my dick for it," he had said. Jenner saw a purity in Sugar that he felt compelled to protect. So, Jenner did what he had to do, and that was the last he ever saw of Sugar.

"I got a ninety-day chip," Garcia said. "And a sponsor. I'm doing good."

"You're a good man, Garcia. Good man."

"I think she'll leave me now. And my sponsor is going to hate me."

"Their loss, my friend."

"Think I can have just a little more?"

"Should take it easy, buddy. Can't slam as much as you were slamming, you know."

"Just a little more, please."

The men cooked up the last of Jenner's gift, and Garcia took in far more than he should have. It wasn't long before he was vomiting and convulsing. Jenner knew he had to find the man some help. He gathered his things and exited the temple.

Across the street, Jenner found a pay phone and dialed 911. "There's a man who needs help," he told them. He hung up the phone and made himself comfortable in the dirty doorway of a shop that wouldn't open for a few more hours. The smell of urine was strong. As the distant sirens grew louder, Jenner closed his eyes for a moment and involuntarily released his bowels.

Jenner's mother is telling him about the birds. "Some birds poop when they hunt."

Jenner giggles.

"Isn't it amazing how our heavenly father built all these creatures with different skills?" his mother says, pushing his hair behind his ears. "You know, one species of heron actually floats bait on the water's surface and waits until its prey rises to eat it, and then the bird munches it all up." She makes a mouth out of her hand and munches on Jenner's belly.

Jenner wants to laugh, but he's disturbed. "But that's mean, Mommy. Those fish come up to eat, and then they die?"

"Oh, honey. The world is full of creatures that must give their lives up so that others may live."

When Jenner awoke, the ambulance was no longer there. He prayed for Garcia but had no time for guilt. In the entryway where Jenner lay, the smell of feces now mingled with the stale stench of urine. He had to get himself cleaned up. The lock on the door behind him clicked. The shopkeeper in the window gave Jenner a dirty look and yelled, "Get out of here before I call the cops."

"Yeah, yeah," Jenner responded to the muffled voice. "Don't get your panties in a wad." Jenner eased himself up and headed toward the lake on the other side of town. He needed a good washing.

Down by the lake's edge, Jenner recognized
a fellow from the neighborhood. His name was
Alfred, and he wasn't quite right in the head. Jenner
never really talked to him, but he saw him around.
Today, Alfred was talking to a piece of wood that
was floating in the water.

Jenner waded out into the lake. He would need
to be underwater to take his pants off and wash
them. He was arrested once for public indecency,
so he was careful. Tonight was not the night to get
arrested—he still had a little party left in him. After
cleaning himself up as best he could, he returned to
the shoreline and lay on the sand, letting the sun dry
him off.

"Name's Alfred," Alfred said as he stood above
Jenner. Jenner opened his eyes to see the man block-
ing the sun.

"Jenner. Nice to meet you."

"You looking for something?" Alfred asked.

"Nope. Just drying off."

"'Cause I got a little something if you're interested."
Alfred pulled a baggy of a powdery white substance
out of his shirt pocket.

"Whatcha got?" Jenner lifted himself up onto his
elbows.

"Stuff."

Jenner put out his hand. "Let me take a look at
that."

"Unh-uh. No way, bucko. Forty-dollar deposit before it touches your hand."

Jenner lay back down. "Then beat it. I don't got no money."

"What do you have?"

"A pair of shit-stained pants and an encyclopedic knowledge of birds."

"Really?" Alfred chewed on his thumb. "You know a lot about birds?"

"Yep."

Alfred grew anxious. "You know a lot about them? 'Cause, I got a hurt one over there." He pointed to an area just beyond the shore where a series of tarps and blankets were draped over a twine clothesline— a makeshift tent. "I live there. There's this sick bird that comes and sees me every night."

"How you know it's sick?"

"I think it's got a drug problem."

Jenner laughed and put his head back down. "Don't we all, my friend. Don't we all?"

Alfred looked at the baggy in his hand. "I'm real worried about this bird." He scratched his head. "Say, what if I give you this stuff and you just come take a look at it, tell me what to do?"

"Where'd you get that stuff?"

"From the bird. I tell you, he's got a drug problem."

Jenner studied Alfred's face. The man wasn't bullshitting him; he really thought he got that shit from the bird. Either way, Jenner was sure whatever the man was holding in his hand would be good enough to get him through the night. "Okay. Show me the bird."

Alfred lifted the tarp and invited Jenner into his home. Just as the man said, inside was a bird—a white heron—next to a nest of chicks. The heron looked at him but didn't move.

Alfred walked over to the bird and ran his hand along the bird's chest. The bird still didn't move. Alfred came back over to Jenner and opened his palm. There, in Alfred's hand, was a white powdery substance. "See, I think the bird has a drug problem."

*Either way, Jenner was sure whatever the man was holding in his hand would be good enough to get him through the night.*

Jenner smiled and patted Alfred on the back. "It's called powder down. They're just really fine feathers that the bird sort of plucks and squashes up to put on sores and stuff. Soaks up the blood. You smoke that shit and ain't nothing going to happen to you, my friend."

"So he's not sick?"

"Well, it's a little strange that she's not flying away from you. That she's got her chicks right here in this hovel with you."

"He's my friend. The bird's my friend." He took the baggy out of his pocket. "Well, here you go. A deal's a deal."

Jenner smiled, took the baggy from Alfred, and walked out from under the tarps. He found a spot under a shady tree and looked at the contents of the baggy a little closer. *What the hell?* he thought. He snorted a little and then sat back and waited to see if anything would happen.

The smell in the hospital that Jenner awoke in was hardly as antiseptic as it could have been. *In fact,* Jenner thought, *it smells downright dirty.* He'd woken up in this hospital before, and each time he battled with feelings of indignant righteousness—this was America, for god's sake, and he had the right to put in his body whatever he wanted to—and feelings of complete worthlessness—why did they even bother to try to save him? The doctor fiddled with something on Jenner's leg before noticing that Jenner's eyes were open.

"Welcome to the world of the living, Mr. Jenner," the doctor said. He covered Jenner's leg with the hospital blanket. "We had to put your IV in your leg. Had some trouble finding a good vein."

"Tell me about it," Jenner said, half joking, half embarrassed.

"I bet you'd like to know why you're here."

"I've got some guesses."

"Your heart's taken a beating, you know."

"A medical degree and a knack for delivering puns?" Jenner said. "Boy, doc, is there anything you can't do?"

"I can't save a dying man who doesn't want to help me do it."

Jenner's head was aching. He closed his eyes, preparing himself for the worn-out lecture about his life choice. *This is where the real suffering takes place*, he thought, *here in their temples of medicine and miracles.*

The doctor scribbled something in Jenner's chart. "I've called in a drug counselor," he said. "To be honest, I doubt it will do any good, but it's hospital policy, so..."

"I know the drill."

The doctor put his hand on Jenner's shoulder. "Hang in there, buddy. Rock bottom's got to be near."

The doctor turned to leave. "Doctor?" Jenner said. "You got me on methadone or something?"

"Or something," the doctor said as he slipped out the door.

Jenner knew it would be at least another few hours before he could leave. He closed his eyes and tried to get some trouble-free sleep.

The bird in Alfred's tent is upset. She is pacing back and forth and moving her head from side to side. Jenner knows there is nothing he can say to make her feel any better, so he sits and tries to comfort her with his eyes. The bird singles out an egg from her nest. Furiously she pecks at its shell until it cracks open. Jenner can see the faint movement of an underdeveloped chick. It moves for a moment and then stops. The bird looks at Jenner. He swears he sees tears in her eyes, but Jenner is positive birds can't cry.

Jenner watched a little television while he waited for the drug counselor. He knew these counselors meant well, but it was all a giant waste of time. Jenner only hoped whatever that doctor gave him would hold him over until he could get out and get some more.

The drug counselor was a pretty blond woman who looked vaguely familiar to Jenner. She introduced herself as Angela and sat down. There were several moments of uncomfortable silence before she spoke again.

"You don't recognize me, do you, Jenner?"

"I know you?" The words were no sooner out of Jenner's mouth before the light of recognition illuminated his face. "Sugar Tits?"

"Angela."

"Oh, right. Sorry." Jenner sat up a little straighter. "How you been?"

"Actually, I've never been better. Doing really good now. Been clean almost two years."

"Good for you, sweetheart. Really. Good for you."

"It's possible, you know. Getting clean."

Jenner smoothed out the hospital blanket that covered his body. He smiled at her.

Angela put her hand on his arm. "You ever think about getting clean?"

Jenner nodded. "I think about winning the lottery and space travel too."

"Your friend Alfred is getting the help he needs."

"Alfred?"

"The guy who found you. Came in with you." Angela poured Jenner a cup of water. "Turns out he's got a loving family that has been worried sick about him. His meds quit working, and he cycled. You bringing him here got him the help he needed."

"That's great, but I didn't do anything."

141

"And I just came from your old friend Garcia's room. You remember him, don't you?"

"Name sounds familiar."

"It should. He says he was with you late last night."

"Angela, sweetheart. I don't mean no disrespect, but can we get on with this so I can get going?"

"He's going to be fine. I think this is exactly what he needed to really solidify his recovery."

Jenner sighed heavily and turned his head toward the window. He knew what she was doing. If logic wouldn't work, certainly guilt might.

"You know what was the final straw that got me clean?" Angela walked to the other side of the bed, putting herself in Jenner's line of sight. Looking him straight in the eye, she said, "Watching you suck that guy's dick."

Jenner sat motionless. He wished he knew what emotion she wanted from him so that he could give it to her and get out of there.

"Not because it made me think less of you, Jenner, but because I couldn't believe you thought I was worth enough to do that. You sacrificed your own dignity for mine. That's when I realized that I must have still had some left."

"I always thought you were worth more than a guy like me could give you."

"That's just it, Jenner. You gave me the most precious gift. You saved me." Angela put her hand on Jenner's. "You saved me, and it is killing me that I can't return the favor."

"I'm glad you're happy, Sugar."

"You're leaving against doctor's orders. The doctor's not sure how long your heart's going to last out there."

"Probably just as long as it would in here."

"There's nothing I can say, is there?"

"Nothing that would keep me in here, but I'd sure love to hear you say you miss me."

Jenner returned to the lake later that night. Alfred's tent had not yet been dismantled. On the bus ride there, Jenner had made a stop at a friend's pad to pick up a little fuel for the night. He made himself at home in Alfred's tent. The bird was gone, but the eggs were still there. Jenner believed he could still save them. He'd keep them warm until they hatched.

Jenner cooked himself his usual meal on a spoon over a lighter. As he fed himself, he planned out his course of action to save those heron chicks' lives. *A little heat, body heat, perhaps*, he thought as he closed his eyes.

Jenner's body felt bad. He sensed it wouldn't hold out much longer. His heart was slowing. *This is the end, isn't it, God?* he thought. *It's been a hell of a ride, I'll tell you that.* Jenner curled himself into a ball, his breathing shallow. *I'm ready, God. Been ready for a long, long time.* Jenner closed his eyes. The white heron was there. Feathered plume standing straight up in the air. He wouldn't have to save the chicks after all. He watched the bird look at him with tearful eyes before he faithfully surrendered to the relentless pull of sleep.

# Going to California
*Megan Guiney*

I keep my television on when I sleep. I turn the sound off, but there's still that heavy, droning buzz. The light never bothers me. Jill asked me to turn it off before we fell asleep last night. "Rob," she whispered. "Rob, can you please shut the TV off? I can't sleep with it on." I remember that I lay there, with my hands tucked behind my head, and I sighed. I stared at her outline—a tiny, curled up ball of blankets, illuminated every now and then by the flash of a commercial. She wasn't facing me. That was my very first night without the television. There wasn't a reassuring buzz to fall asleep to. Just snoring. I didn't know that girls of her size were capable of such noise. Before I met her, I really didn't know that girls snored at all.

She wakes up before me when she stays over. Sometimes I like to watch her get ready for work. Jill has a strict schedule for everything in her life. Every morning she lays out her clothes, showers, brushes her teeth, dries her hair, puts on her clothes and makeup, and then makes coffee. In that order. She gives herself exactly forty-five minutes for this ritual, and any minor change completely throws off her day. I usually pretend I'm asleep, but today through half-closed eyes, I watch her walk around the apartment. She's so put-together. She makes me feel like a grown-up.

She walks into my bedroom, clutching a cup of coffee under her nose. After setting the cup on the nightstand, she climbs back into bed and snuggles up beside me. I breathe in the smell of her shampoo. It smells like apples.

"Morning, baby," she says. "It's raining outside." I pull a pillow over my face, groaning. Jill playfully pushes it away and laughs. She's got a great smile. Lots of very white, very straight teeth. "C'mon, get up. You have work." She kisses me on the forehead and stands up. The room is cold, and everything seems washed over in a grayish-blue tone. I hate rainy days. Jill walks over to my computer to put on some music. "I'll see you later, all right?"

I stay in bed after she leaves. I work at a music store in Downtown Crossing, and my shift doesn't start for another two hours. I close my eyes, trying to block out the blue room. The computer becomes quiet, changing songs. A few chords quietly fill the room. A Zeppelin classic, my favorite. It's funny how a certain song or simple guitar strum can bring back a whole world of memories, stuff you didn't even mean to remember.

It was one of those nights that are a little hazy.
You know you had a great time, even if you only remember tiny fragments. I don't really remember how
or why we started talking. I have this image, though.
I can't shake it. A dimly lit room with a few people
strewn about on couches and rugs. Discarded cups
roll by, listlessly drifting over the sticky hardwood
floor. A partially open window and a long, thin
curtain swaying in the breeze. And Amy. Amy's a
girl that a guy like me would never dream of just
going up to. A girl that would never cast a glance
in my direction. But it happened. I don't remember
making the decision to talk to her or feeling my
stomach churn as I walked near. All of a sudden, we
were talking. She had been leafing through a stack
of CDs: a collection of homemade compilations
with trite Sharpie-scribbled titles. *Summer 2006.*
*Rainy-day Mix.* We continue to make these CDs as
a way to define a period of time. We don't remember
every detail, but the songs define the moments we
do remember, rather than our memories shaping our
selection of songs. We make soundtracks for our
lives.

Amy chose to listen to "Going to California," the
song playing in my room right now. She led me
out to the side yard, pulled up her long skirt, and
expertly climbed the thick branches of an oak tree.
I remember catching her eye as she looked down

from her perch. A huge smile, one like I've never seen before or since. We shared a branch. The song, combined with muffled voices and the low chatter of crickets in the background, eased out of the window. The air was humid, and a warm breeze blew through Amy's long blond hair. A few strands fell into her face. She didn't brush them away. She clumsily kicked her feet as they dangled from the branch, stirring the dark turquoise folds of her skirt.

She leaned back against the trunk and closed her eyes. "I just love this song," she murmured. As she tapped her fingers on the branch, Zeppelin's lyrics passed through her lips in a throaty, low voice. "Made up my mind to make a new start, going to California with an aching in my heart..." She smiled.

"Sounds good, doesn't it? Just picking up and starting all over, somewhere new. Somewhere more exciting."

"Yeah, I guess," I said. "I've never been out there before. I kinda like it here, though. It's what I'm used to." My mind was already reeling ahead to fantasies of our summer together, walking on the beach and listening to music in my car. We sat in comfortable silence, mentally inhabiting entirely different worlds. I didn't know it then. I figured we were both imagining the same sunset. Amy raised her head and looked right into my eyes. She was close enough to touch.

"You know, it's funny," she said. "Here we are, sitting in a tree and talking, and I don't even know your name. And yet I feel like I could say anything. Don't you think that's funny?"

I want to believe that I replied with something clever. I want to believe that I made her laugh out loud with my wit. But I remember this part clearly. And I don't remember laughter. Not the good kind, anyway.

"It's Rob," I replied. "I'm Rob." I might as well have stiffly hit my chest, pointing and barking: "Me, Tarzan. You, Jane."

"Rob," she whispered slowly, as if tasting the word for the first time. "I'm Amy. It's nice to meet you." She started to laugh, a clear, infectious laugh that made my chest ache. Are girls aware of these little moments? These moments that make a guy pause, in awe of something so natural and beautiful and real.

What happened next is a bit blurry. I remember hearing a girl drunkenly shriek Amy's name, drowning out the music and voices and crickets. Amy was suddenly on the ground, peering up at me through the branches with those bright eyes. "It really was nice to meet you," she said, wrapping an arm around the trunk of the tree. She grinned, waved, and was gone. And I was drunk, alone, and stuck in a tree.

We never talked to one another again after that night. I think I saw her at graduation, but I couldn't really tell. Northeastern is a big school. Everyone has blond hair.

I work at Strawberries on Washington Street. It's a huge store, shiny and tall and gray. I worked here all through college. It's hard not to be elitist when you work at a music store. Music is just one of those things that people love to be snobby about. What you listen to says a lot about who you are, or so we think. It defines someone's lifestyle and personality, most of the time.

"Hey, Rob, what's up?" Joey is running in my direction. I shouldn't say running. It's more of an exaggerated step. He kind of hunches his shoulders up and hits the floor hard with each slow move. He's sixteen, a little punk, but a good kid mostly.

"Hey, Joey." I watch him bend down and rub dirt off of his sneaker. They're new, some kind of sneaker designed to make you jump higher or whatever.

"What the hell," he mutters. "I just got these, and they're already fuckin' dirty." I ignore him and continue to pretend I'm organizing CDs. I like being on the floor so I can watch customers. People buying music are funny. Choosing a CD is a private thing, but people are aware that others can see them. Everyone picks up and examines the CDs that they think will make them look a certain way. And when they think no one's looking, they'll linger and rummage for a band or singer they secretly love.

Today I'm watching one guy in particular. He's middle-aged, clinging to a few greasy strands of hair. He's probably on his lunch break. He's been hovering around the first few letters of the alphabet in the Rock/Pop section. Plenty of bands to choose from. He's managed to touch every CD without looking interested. Until now. He stops rummaging. He casts his eyes quickly to the left and then to the right. No one's around. He picks up the CD, and an almost imperceptible smirk lifts the corners of his mouth. He's found it.

"Phil Collins? Is he fuckin' kidding me?" Joey's voice cracks next to me. He gets legitimately angry when people don't have the same taste he does. He takes it really seriously, almost as if he's getting paid to talk trash about bad musicians.

"I know, right?" I look over to the front of the store and watch one of my coworkers put up a new poster. Some new singer/dancer. She's sitting backwards in a chair, with a seductive look and her long hair draped over one eye. The CD's name is written in deliberately messy silver letters. *Fantasy.* Joey follows my gaze. "That girl is hot," he decides. He squints, trying to get a better look.

I shake my head. "Nah, not my type."

"Whaddya mean, not your type? She's a hot girl. She's every guy's type."

"That's bullshit. I just don't like her."

"What, you don't like brown hair? Doesn't your girlfriend have brown hair?" I nod, picturing Jill's neat, straight, short brown hair. It's always exactly in place, even when she wakes up.

"It's not her hair. She looks fake. It's all airbrushed."

Joey shrugs. "Whatever, man. I just like looking." He walks away, fishing through his pocket for his cell phone. I go on break and sit in the back room, reading the *Globe*. I leaf through, searching for the music section. I scan a few new CD reviews.

At the bottom of the page, there's a transcript of an interview. And Amy's picture. She's right there, in my hands. She lives in L.A. now and apparently has a gig coming up. I read one of her comments.

*Yeah, I love it out here. I needed a change from Boston. I was getting a little bored, ya know? L.A. has a bigger crowd, lots of different people. I'm planning on staying here indefinitely.*

I throw the paper back onto a desk. I never took a chance with her after that night. I figured she'd just wander back into my life somehow. I mean, nights like that don't happen all the time. And then Jill came along. She's great and all, but sometimes I wonder. Right now, I'm obviously not drunk, I'm not alone, and I'm definitely not stuck in a tree. But that doesn't stop me from wishing I was.

# Drive
*Danielle Rollins*

My father taught me to drive in Utah, on a highway just before sunrise, when the air was so crisp and cold that it burned through my lungs every time I inhaled. He unrolled all of our windows, and the early desert air seeped in and made us shiver. I was only fifteen and everything about our old Buick—from the lemon-scented air freshener to the velvet-covered seats to the low purr of the engine beneath my legs—made me feel grown up. Daddy looked over at me and winked. He shifted the car out of park, and the corners of his eyes got crinkly and wrinkled like they always do when he's excited.

"Floor it," he said. I gripped the steering wheel as hard as I could, closed my eyes, and pressed down on the gas. For a second, nothing happened. Then the car jolted forward, and we were flying down the highway. That's just what it felt like, flying.

Now I hold the wheel steady with three fingers, resting my hand on my knee as I steer. It's almost seventeen years later, and I'm right back where I started, driving through the cliffs of Utah with the highway straight and endless before me.

It's raining tonight, and all I can see of it is the wet glare off the black road. Sometimes a stray drop spits in through the passenger side window, which I've kept open because the stale smell of my car's air conditioning and the day-old fast food makes me feel nauseous. I rest my head against the car seat and rub my eyes with my free hand; I move my thumb and forefinger in slow circles, as though that will push the sleep from my eyes. The motel isn't far ahead; already I can see the fluorescent glow of its vacancy light buzzing in the darkness, illuminating a building that looks exactly like the postcard I've folded into quarters and shoved in my side pocket. It's one of nearly a dozen postcards my mother sent to Dad's old apartment, unaware that he'd lost his battle with lung cancer nearly five years ago.

I loosen my grip on the steering wheel and shift in my seat. The vinyl seat cover squeaks against my jeans, and a spasm of pain shoots up my back. I've always been stick thin, built like my dad. I don't have the padding to make the long, cross-country trips comfortable. I ease down on the brake, wrapping my toes around the pedal. I took off my cowboy boots about sixty miles back, when they started making my calves and the arches of my feet sting with pain. They sit on the passenger seat next to me, the leather smelling of the olive oil that I polish them with and the sweat from my feet and legs.

I pull up outside the motel and put the car into park. I pull the boots on over my bare feet, enjoying

the feel of the butter-soft leather against my skin. The parking lot is empty. She must've already gone—if she'd been here at all.

The motel clerk looks about seventeen and has the widest, flattest, blackest face I have ever seen. His skin glistens beneath the yellow hotel lights, and the only spots of color on his face are the red-tinged whites of his eyes.

"You need room?" His voice is tainted with a heavy accent that I cannot place. He barely glances at me before his eyes flit back to the seven-inch television on the other side of the glass partition.

"Um, yeah." I reach into the canvas backpack slung over my shoulder and sift around the extra socks and underwear before my fingers enclose a roll of cash bound by a rubber band. I peel off two twenties and slide them across the counter. "Just tonight, please."

The clerk's program switches to a commercial; a department store jingle blares out of the tiny television set. A dancing reindeer holds a sign advertising 10 percent off before Christmas. The clerk turns back to face me. There's a plastic nametag that reads *Melvin* attached to his shirt.

"You are visiting family?" Melvin takes the money from the counter and turns in his chair until he is facing a computer that looks at least twenty years old. The keyboard is gray with dirt, and the keys stick when he types.

"Something like that."

"You grew up here?"

"Just passing through." I turn my back to him and face the door that looks out onto the empty parking lot.

I've never known how to answer that question. I didn't grow up anywhere. I spent my childhood driving across the highways between Nevada and West Virginia with my dad. I slept most nights in a bucket seat with my cheek plastered against the passenger side window, the cornfields of Nebraska or Iowa or Kansas speeding past my head, separated only by the cold glass.

"Is there food nearby?" I ask. "A Denny's or..."

"There's a diner. Across the street."

"Phone?"

He turns in his chair and points to a hallway just behind him. I pull my backpack farther up my shoulder. The heels of my boots click against the tile floors as I walk.

"Nice boots." Melvin nods at my feet.

"My mother's," I say. I was only seven when I woke up, before dawn, to see my closet door ajar, the leather tips of her boots peeking out, as though they were afraid to enter my room without permission.

"She must have been a stylish lady."

"Must've been." My voice is quieter than I intend. My mother was stylish. I hold on to this knowledge, place it with the other things I know about her. So few things. She would sit on our front porch with a beer and watch thunderstorms as intensely as if they'd had a plot. Her hair was the color of dead grass. She loved to drive more than she loved anything else in the world.

She had this '72 Mercedes, light blue with dark leather interior. It was the most impractical car. It would break down every other week, but she wouldn't get rid of it. She used to take it out late at night and drive around the city just to see the way the lights looked in the dark. Sometimes I wouldn't hear the rumble of her engine pulling back into our driveway until early in the morning, when silver-blue light was drifting in through my windows.

Then, one night, she didn't come back. Dad bought the old Buick Skylark the next day, taking out a loan that he would never repay and that I got saddled with when he died. I'd read in the seat next to him, studying school textbooks for exams I would never take while he drove across the country— searching motel parking lot after motel parking lot for the car that she loved.

I cross the lobby to the pay phone in the corner. The plastic earpiece is warm against my skin, as though someone else had just put it down. I drop two quarters into the coin slot, listen to them clink inside the machine, and try not to practice what I'm going to say when someone answers.

The phone rings twice. A girl's voice comes on the line: "Hello?"

I run my tongue over my lip, and the skin is dry and flaky. Melvin's television program is on again. Someone tells a joke that I can't hear, and the laugh track booms through the empty lobby.

"Hello?" she says again.

I place the phone back on the receiver, pull my backpack farther up my shoulder, and head out the front door into the rain.

I walk into the diner and sit in a booth near the door. The counter is yellow, and the linoleum peels at the edges. I spread my hands out on top of it so my fingers cover the cracks that spider-web out from the center. The light in the diner has a blue sheen that makes everyone's skin look translucent, pale. The highway runs next to my window. I can't hear the rumble of the cars outside, but they make the plastic booth vibrate. Their headlights flash white in the diner as they drive past.

The diner is generic—like the backdrop of an old fifties movie. A tall counter circles around a wide window that opens into the kitchen. The chalkboard above the kitchen says *Fiesta Night* in bright blue and orange colors. There are tiny sombreros on all of the tables, and the diner smells like nacho cheese and beans instead of fries.

The waitress is young, maybe seventeen, with greasy hair that hangs next to her face in clumps. She's wearing a garish yellow uniform that's starting to go gray, probably from years of being washed with black shirts and jeans.

"Just coffee," I say before she can remove the notebook from the pocket in the front of her apron. She nods and sets a mug on my table. It's white with a green handle, and when she pours the coffee it sloshes over the rim and spills onto the table, making a brown ring on the linoleum when she moves the mug away.

"God, sorry." She uses the edge of her apron to wipe the coffee from the table.

"How much?" There's change at the bottom of my backpack; I feel like a teenager as I dig for it, pulling out socks and postcards along with quarters and nickels. The waitress makes a noise—like half a sigh, soft and a little breathy—and picks at something lying among a pile of receipts that I've just rescued from the mess.

"Is she yours?"

Her finger is resting on a wallet-sized photograph. It's of Gracie when she was only a year and a half old. Her wispy hair is hidden by a floppy yellow hat that she's trying to pull off with one chubby fist. The photographer got her to laugh by putting a Winnie the Pooh stuffed animal on top of the camera. I can see two teeth between her parted lips.

"Yeah." I pick up the photograph and lean to one side so I can slide it into the back pocket of my jeans.

"How old?"

"Two."

The waitress parts her lips. She's going to ask something else, but then her gaze falls to the second finger on my left hand. It's been bare since last week, when I searched through the yellow pages of some forgotten town until I found a pawnshop and traded the ring for enough cash to last six more weeks on the road. I can see how I look to her: the forgotten photograph, the absent husband. She closes her mouth and chews on her lip.

"Um, a dollar sixty."

I put two dollars on the table. She thanks me and leaves.

I touch the finger, making a ring with my middle finger and thumb around the skin that connects it to my hand. It feels natural bare, more natural than when it held the ring—gaudy and obtrusive. Never my own.

I met John when I was in college. I was on the shoulder of a highway, sitting next to my old Ford truck with a flat tire. John pulled over when he saw me. His clothes were clean and carefully pressed. There were creases ironed into the sleeves of his shirt and down the front of his dark pants; but he said nothing when the fabric near his knee tore on the highway gravel or when the oil from my tire left dark marks on his perfect white sleeves.

We'd only been dating for five months when he proposed. I said no the first time—and the second.

But then we took a road trip to visit some friends. There was a snowstorm and a cheap motel and we drank the tiny, six-dollar bottles of white Zinfandel from the mini fridge and undressed each other with clumsy fingers and stumbled when we tried to make it to the bed. I remember the next part the best, of course. Three weeks later I was in the bathroom at John's apartment. It had been eight days since my missed period. I sat on the floor with my legs stretched across the room so I could touch the other wall with my big toe. The tile was cold through my underwear, and goose bumps spread over my legs and up the back of my neck. I held the plastic applicator between my thumb and forefinger, and I closed my eyes when the pink line appeared, telling me I was no longer alone in my body.

*I closed my eyes when the pink line appeared, telling me I was no longer alone in my body.*

The next time he proposed, I said yes. For a while there were baby showers and bridesmaids, churches and white dresses, and rattles tied in pink bows. Then, in a wave of pain and screaming, Gracie arrived and everything changed. I didn't know how to change diapers or breast-feed. I didn't know how to stop her from crying. I'd forget to buckle her car seat when we drove to the grocery store or to the post office. I didn't know. I never had a mother.

It's still raining when I leave the diner. It's cold, slushy rain that hints of snow. I pull my thin sweater tighter around my shoulders and wait until there's a lull in the traffic to dodge across the street, not wanting to walk up the block to the crosswalk. The rain leaves dark, wet spots on my sweater; it soaks through to my skin.

I see it when I cross the parking lot to throw away some of the receipts from my bag in the dumpster near the alley. It's hidden behind the dumpster and a tree with no leaves that stretches almost as high as the motel itself. It's sky blue—just like I remembered—though the paint is rusting around the headlights and on the back bumper. The interior is just as beautiful as it was when I was seven years old.

I drop the receipts, and some of them stick to the gravel at my feet and turn gray where the rain hits them. Two blow away, bouncing across the parking lot in the wind. I wrap a hand around the strap of my backpack, twisting it so tightly around my finger that the finger gets cold and turns purple around the nail. Then I stumble toward the lobby. It's not until

I'm inside that I realize how cold I was, how my ears and nose burn.

"She's here?" I ask. "The woman who owns that car?"

Melvin looks up from the television. "I am sorry, I..."

"The woman who owns the blue Mercedes. It's the only other car in the parking lot. Which room is she in?"

"I don't think..."

"Which room!"

"Thirty-seven, but..."

The hallway is dim; the overhead light is flickering. My footsteps are muffled by the thin brown carpet that stops two inches before the wall, revealing cold burnt red and orange tiles. Someone turns on a vacuum; the whir of its engine is loud but far away, maybe on a different floor.

I walk faster. I'm reading the numbers on the doors—27, 25, 23. My approach is soundless until I reach the door to the stairway; the carpet gives way to concrete. I leave behind the dim overhead lamps for buzzing fluorescent lights. My boots thunder against the concrete. I walk faster. My hand barely skims the cold, metal handrail. The stairway is filled with the noise of my approach.

I reach the third floor. There's a housekeeper's cart at the end of the hall. Something inside of me constricts, and I lift my hand to my chest. I wrap my hand around the collar of my sweater, rolling the plastic buttons between my finger and thumb.

"No." I form the word with my tongue and my mouth, but I don't say it out loud. I start to run. The tile beneath the thin carpet sends a jolt through my legs and knees. I keep running toward the cart at the end of the hall. The cart in front of her room.

"Mom?"

A boy with acne and long blond hair is making the bed inside her room. His pale hands are so thin that when he tucks the comforter beneath the mattress he doesn't have to lift it. I stop at the door, and he looks up. He takes his hands out from under the mattress and places them on top of the bed so that only one corner of the comforter is tucked in and the other falls at an odd angle across the box spring.

"Are you Mary?"

His eyes are big. Blue. I nod, and he jumps up from the floor, rubbing his hands together as he crosses the room.

"She left this for you."

He drops a key into my hand. It's big and old-fashioned looking—not really like a car key at all.

"She isn't here?" I ask.

"Left about an hour ago. Taxi."

I sit on the corner of the bed and look out the window. The sleet has gotten thicker; it almost looks

white, like snow. I turn the key over in my hand and wrap my fingers around it so tight that it cuts into my skin.

"Um, I need to go get more towels. I'll be back." The boy claps his hands together once and walks out into the hall.

I bite my lip and try to focus on the pain, but the memories pour in anyway. I know very little about my mother, but I know we're the same. I'm just like her.

We had been fighting, John and I. Yelling. He called me a bad mother. I said that I was suffocating.

Gracie was crying. She was two years old then, but I held her like she was an infant. I took her to the car so I could drive until she fell asleep, like I did when she was a baby. John was yelling after me, but I didn't hear him. As soon as I wrapped my hands around the wheel, I was free. I was home.

I was just going to go around the block, and then I was going to go back and talk to John. I was going to fix things. I wanted to fix things.

But the drive was intoxicating; I couldn't stop. I drove like my mother did when I was young. I drove to escape the suburbs, my family. I drove to remind myself of all the places I could go. Gracie started laughing, so I went faster. All I could think about was the speed. All I wanted to do was drive.

And we drove faster, taking curves at fifty until her laughs bubbled over and grew louder. Until she was screaming with laughter.

Sixty. Seventy.

And I didn't see the van—the green van that matched the trees and didn't have its lights on.

I learned to drive on the highway.

And I'd forgotten the things John had said and the things I had said. I had forgotten everything but the laughter and the feel of the wheel, sweaty and vibrating, under my fingers.

Felt like flying.

And I didn't see the van back out onto the road. The car shook. Gracie was screaming, and I was holding the wheel so tight, trying to keep us steady, trying to keep us steady.

We hit a tree. I was fine. But I went to the hospital. I drank cheap coffee in Styrofoam cups, and I sat on the plastic chairs in the waiting room and read articles that I don't remember from *Newsweek* and *Sports Illustrated*. I walked to the other side of the room, behind the fish tank, and waited there when John arrived to speak to the doctor.

His daughter had been in an accident. She would be fine.

She wasn't wearing her seat belt.

The driver was going over seventy.

She was badly injured.

But she would be fine.

I waited until I heard those words a second time. Then I took the keys and drove.

I drove for seven years.

I put the key on my lap. There's a phone on the nightstand in the corner of her room. I lean over the bed and pick up the handset. I dial the numbers I know by heart.

She answers on the first ring. "Hello?"

I cup my hand around the receiver and close my eyes. Her voice is so close, I hear her breathing.

She clears her throat, and I can hear a shuffle, like she's moving. A door closes.

"Mom?" she asks.

I've imagined what it would be like for her to say that word. Every day for seven years I've imagined it. It throws me off guard. For a minute I think about what it would be like if I spoke. Can all of this be undone? Can words send you back in time? For a minute this thought fills me, as though by magic. Then the minute passes, and I put the receiver back in its cradle.

I pick up my mother's key and turn it over in my hands. The metal is warm, like she kept it in the pocket of her jeans or her coat. Outside the rain has

turned to snow, and it's falling harder, blanketing
the roads. There's another postcard in my backpack.
She won't be there; it's not her style to go back,
but I'll go anyway. It's somewhere to go. I'll leave
tonight to stay ahead of the weather. It'll be a long
drive.

# Youth Issue

# Editor's Note

Many artists of both the written word and visual art hesitate when asked how old they were when they started to create. When exactly did it happen, that shift from dreamer to creator? Is there even a shift—or are we always dreamers and creators simultaneously?

In support of that early discovery of the creator's role, each year *Ink-Filled Page* dedicates one quarterly issue to talented young writers and artists. All the work you'll find on the following pages is created by artists in grades six through twelve—though you'd never guess that these creators have any less life experience than other *Ink-Filled Page* contributors. Their voices are strong, their themes are mature, and their use of literary and artistic devices shows mastery in connecting with the audience.

Revel in the talent on these pages. Remember the creators' names. Surely, you'll see them again as they continue the path of turning dreams into creations.

—Ali McCart

# The Orange that Got Eaten and His Thoughts Along the Way
## *Malia Wagner (Age 16)*

Being the last orange in the fruit bowl brought great loneliness for the solitary Florida fruit. Day after day his thoughts were absorbed by the awful scent of Lysol that always seemed to linger in the air, and if there was ever a moment he could get his mind off the horrible stench, he would find himself thinking of the human, stalking happily through her chemically spotless home. It was almost a relief, actually—anything to keep the smell of sterilization out of his mind. Of course, next to Lysol, the human was probably the least comforting thing he could think of.

From the time he bloomed into a flower on the orange tree, he'd heard tales concerning the fate of oranges. Oranges almost never got to live a full life. It was a sad truth, but one the last orange in the fruit bowl had chosen to ignore at a young age. The elder oranges would tell legends about oranges picked in the prime of their lives from their mother trees and shipped to grocery stores in horrid places— places that were cold and wet, or dry and hot, or even worse: places so humid oxygen could barely get through the skin of the much-beloved fruit. "They suffocated there," the elders, older oranges who spent their days listening to the conversations of humans around them, said, "which might be better than the fate befalling those who live to be...chosen."

*Chosen* was a dangerous word around the orange tree. The elders related horrible stories heard from the lips of the enemy, telling in great detail how their brethren were shipped to the grocery stores. The humans, with their large hands and long fingers, would handpick the oranges they wanted to eat. They would squeeze them to see if they were too ripe, or not ripe enough. And when the time came... knives, blood, teeth, gnawing, gnashing—the most painful of painful deaths.

For a long time the orange was sure that the stories of humans eating oranges were just myths, just stories the old oranges clung to in order to frighten the newer arrivals to the grocery bin, but he had seen it for himself now. It was no myth, it was real. And it was only a matter of time until he too would be eaten.

The sun was high in the sky, and the last orange in the fruit bowl was worried. The human kept looking at him hungrily, moving him from place to place,

trying to decide whether she wanted to eat him now
or not. Her fingers scraped against his shining skin,
nails just barely digging into his peel. She pulled
him out of the fruit bowl, dispensed him back into
the fruit bowl. The suspense was driving him insane.

*If you're going to eat me*, he thought, *just do it now
so I don't have to keep wondering when my moment will
come!*

The stories he had heard haunted him mercilessly.
He could almost feel his skin being pulled off his
body, almost see
the human de-
lightfully licking
her fingers as his
blood squirted
into her mouth.
Over and over,
he'd seen other
oranges have the
blood squeezed

out of them and devoured, bit by painful bit. At
night, as the white, Lysol-laden kitchen glistened,
the lone orange would hear them yelling in pain,
crying for mercy, for help, even for forgiveness. He
could scarcely ever get a peaceful moment because
of the ceaseless scenes. Though it brought him pain
constantly, the orange felt strangely accepting of this

fate; it was to be expected, he had recently learned, for a commercially grown Florida Orange.

Suddenly, he felt the human's hand gripping him. He screamed in terror as the human brought him to the cutting board. Instead of looking him over as she had done before, she immediately pierced and ripped off a bit of his skin. Yelping in pain, he tried to roll away, but she had her hand on him firmly. She calmly tore off half of his skin in one swift motion. He was in such agony he barely even noticed when more of his skin came off, but the horrible stinging of the Lysol-filled air on his bare flesh demanded his attention.

The Lysol. What a horrible way to die, skin burning with Lysol. Cruel, unusual punishment—for weeks the stuff had been suffocating him, making him dizzy with hatred and the utmost annoyance, and now it surrounded him in his last moments, oozing into the deepest craters of his being.

Wailing in tortured dolor, he saw out of the corner of his eye a knife. Though he had little time to study it, it appeared sharper than he had imagined. The knife started toward him, and the world slowed down. He saw it inching forward in the midst of his tormenting woe. It came closer and closer until he felt it slice through him. He expected everything to go black just then and for the agony to stop, but to his horror, it continued. He could feel it slicing down, passing through one of his seeds. The human pulled the knife out and again started cutting him, in fourths this time. She dragged the knife down slowly, carefully, muttering something about needing more oranges from the store next time she went. The last orange in the fruit bowl, now lying on the cutting board, braced for the end as the pain continued to shoot through the four slices.

One of his slices squirted blood onto the human's fingers and she delightfully licked it off, just as he had imagined. She picked the orange up and brought him to her mouth.

*I wonder why humans think oranges taste so good....*

# Capsule
## *Ian Sanquist (Age 18)*

October 7th

Dear Mom,

The vandals smashed more windows at my school last night. They probably won't ever get fixed. My teacher duct taped butcher paper over them, but we can still feel a draft. What do they think they can achieve by smashing windows at our school? They're like those thugs who come into Dad's store and smash all the little models. What do they get out of it? Instead of stealing things to sell or keep, which I can at least understand, they're just breaking things for the sake of breaking them.

A few weeks ago, some kids I go to school with went to the courthouse with a pipe bomb. One of their friends was in detention awaiting trial, so they destroyed the courtroom he was scheduled to be tried in. I don't get it. Why didn't they go to the detention center and blow a hole in the wall to get their friend out, which may have actually worked? As if the justice system is just going to roll over and say, "Since there's no longer a courtroom to try you in, you can go free now." A lot of people at school seem to know who's behind the bombing, but nobody's saying. I'm not sure I would say even if I did know. All my friends would ostracize me, and people I've never even met would come up to me just so they could say things like "Snitches get stitches, bitch." No one was hurt in the attack, and the less I know, the better off I'll probably be. Although if I knew who was behind the subway bombings, I'd turn them in straight away. Trains are never on time anymore.

Remember before you left when we took the train out to the beach? It was such a foggy day,

the skyscrapers all disappeared into the sky. I remember asking you why we would go to the beach on such a dreary day, but you insisted. By the time we got there, the sun had come out and burned off all the fog. It turned out to be the nicest day in months. You were right, like you always were. Today was another foggy day. Even foggier than that one day. After school—I don't know why—I took the train out to that beach. There was no sun this time, though. The fog was thicker out there than in the city, so thick and humid it felt hard to breathe. I wonder if this is what the air could be like in the Arae planetary system, if there even is any air there.

Dad told me that there are people going farther than you. He said that some are going more than a thousand light years away. When I asked him how long it would take to travel a light year, he said, "If you're traveling the speed of light, then it takes a year." I asked him what if you were traveling eighty thousand miles per hour. He didn't know. I found out that the speed of light is 670,616,629 miles per hour, but I couldn't figure out how to compute any- thing beyond that. Even my physics teacher couldn't tell me. Dad said that you would know the answer. How long does it take for a spaceship traveling at eighty thousand miles per hour to go a light year?

The closer you get to the edge of our solar system, the longer it takes for light from the sun to reach your ship, but when I press Send on this e-mail, it will instantly transfer to the inbox of your ship's computer. Of course, I know you won't see it for centuries. You won't see any of my e-mails until long after I'm dead, when you reach the Arae system and are unfrozen. This makes me wonder what the point of your mission is. By the time you arrive, everyone down at mission control who approved this voyage will be buried, and your expedition will just be some anachronism. Something left over from this current era of space exploration. Your mission will be forgotten in a decade. What will it be like hundreds of years from now, when you wake up in a strange new place and everyone back down on Earth has forgotten the excitement of watching all those shuttles launch? You'll step out of your ship onto the planet, but the mission will be so old that no one will remember.

But then, even if they don't remember, I suppose they'll still pay attention when the missions start to land. When you astronauts emerge from stasis and broadcast back to Earth, "We have arrived," of course people will pay attention. All it will take is an old newsreel to remind everyone of the days when space expeditions were launched constantly. *Remind* is not the right word. No one will have any recollection at all of those days, of these days. Expeditions are still launched almost daily. The president continues to inflate our national debt exponentially, justifying the missions by pointing out what he calls the pressing need to lay claim to the unexplored parts of space—isn't the universe infinite anyway?—before the Chinese can. Unfortunately, now that they've found out we're competing with

them for sections of dark matter, the Chinese have
requested that we begin to repay our towering debt.

By the time you read this e-mail, our nation's
current problems will be irrelevant. However, the
national fervor that arises when you and all the
other astronauts reach your destinations will be
something akin to the opening of a time capsule.
Buried, forgotten, and dug up so many years later as
a nice surprise for all the people of the future (your
present). So why not fill your capsule with letters
from the current present, the present that existed
around the time when your mission and all the deep
space missions were launched? This present, that to
you, when you wake, will seem at first to be the very
near future, and that the people of the future will
know as the distant past, but that to me is just the
here and the now. I'm not sure if that makes sense.
Regardless of whether or not it does, know that I
will fill your capsule, Mom. Though you are frozen
and rapidly approaching the reaches of our galaxy,
I still think of you, and I doubt there will ever be a
time when you are very far from my thoughts.

And so, with the ever-present knowledge that my
letters will never be answered, I write to you from
Earth, the planet that you were not satisfied to make
your life on. I like to think that perhaps when you
arrive in the Arae system and open your inbox filled
with these e-mails, that perhaps they will anchor

you in some way, serve as a sort of ground control for you. Nothing will be as it was except for me. In the new and unfamiliar world that you are reborn into, I will be there as a disembodied voice that I hope you will always love and recognize.

Your son,
William

November 2<sup>nd</sup>

Dear Mom,

Someone from NASA came to my school today. There was an assembly and he talked about the current missions. He mentioned almost all of them, but he left yours out, so I asked about it. He acted as if he didn't know what I was talking about. Very slowly, I spelled it out for him: the Arae planetary system, the mission that my mom's on. He said something vague to indicate that any information on an expedition to Arae was of the confidential variety. I got kind of mad and said something like, "C'mon, quit making me look like a jerk in front of everyone," which probably just made me look like even more of a jerk. I guess he decided he was done taking questions, because he moved on to pitching the exciting career opportunities that awaited us at NASA. Filling our heads with images of stars and planets, the rings of Saturn, the great gas giants, nebulas at the far reaches of our galaxy and beyond, all of these things which we could see up close in mere years if we signed up now and began training immediately. Before we even graduate from high school, we could be training. After school, during school, before school, on the weekends. Some saw this as a great infringement on their time and said forget it. Others saw only the great voyage that lay before them and put their names down instantly.

Is this how you joined? Did someone come to your school and seduce you with this romantic notion of a space opera? I can't imagine that it would be like that, not for your mission anyway. Your tri-century mission, frozen in suspended animation where you can't even observe the stars and the planets. In the midst of the constellations, you are unbreathing and unaware. Why did you go up there? Did you have a choice? Surely you had a choice. But why would you choose to leave all that you knew so far behind? Why go so deep into space, so deep that the NASA recruiter didn't even bother to mention your mission?

Every one of us has a trajectory. Our own path that we take through life. Trajectories can meet, can be thrown off course, can end up in completely different places than we intended, but we all have one. Each trajectory is unique to the person. We are all our own mission control. It can take directions we never saw coming, for better or for worse. Planets all have trajectories too, and I'm not talking about their orbits around the sun. What's important to remember is that no trajectory is a straight line. Only after reaching the end can any of us look over our trajectory and see exactly where it took us and how it got us there. But you always had a mission, didn't you, Mom? You always knew you wanted to go into space. So then why Dad? Why me? If you always knew you were going to go into space and never return, why did you affect Dad's life and create mine? Unless never returning hadn't originally been a part of your plan. Was that an unexpected divergence from your path? Or was it Dad and I, were we both just deviations along your trajectory?

*But you always had a mission, didn't you, Mom?*

I want to know what your plan was, Mom. But I never can know and you never told me before you left. When you get this e-mail, I want you to respond to it. Maybe somehow the message will find its way into the ether and find me, put me at rest, answer this question which has long itched just under my skin. It will find its way to me and clear my uncertainties, my doubts, my confusion, my eternal curiosity.

Your son,
William

December 17th

Dear Mom,

The moon had a corona around it last night. A fully dilated silvery pupil up in the sky with a pale white iris fringing it. My friends and I spent an hour in the park lying on our backs staring up at it, talking about the infinite possibilities that space represented. Grant was saying that he wants to get off this planet and go up there. Partly to beat the Chinese, but mostly just because he wants to explore the infinite above. He signed up with NASA when they came to school.

I saw the man in the moon, but his face kept changing. Sometimes he was smiling at me, sometimes leering, sometimes he was laughing jovially, laughing with me, but other times at me. His face just kept morphing. Later I hailed a cab and told him to take us to the moon. All the cars looked like spaceships. Last night any of them could've flown us through the top layer of the atmosphere, out beyond the exosphere, where there was ice last night. As we walked through an alley we came across this grubby little alien-like dog. It made weird scarfing noises and moved strangely, burrowing under a fence. We couldn't see its eyes under all the dirty fur. One of my friends wanted to bring it along and make it our companion for the night, but the rest of us were too scared by it.

At one point I was peeing on a fire hydrant on a main street. Someone told me that there was a person looking my way. I asked where and looked over my shoulder to see the guy standing half a block down and said, "Well he isn't saying anything, so fuck him."

When we were at the park, I went over to the playground where there were woodchips on the ground. The woodchips formed fractals that pointed in all different directions, and it was cold enough that they had frozen over, so they sparkled like gold dust. Up in the sky, the air was clear and the stars shone bright, until about two, when fog rolled in, and it became like the Moors, all misty and shrouded.

On some anonymous street, there was a house that looked just like the White House. Grant pinpointed the spot for me with the GPS in his phone, so that

I could come back during daylight hours and take pictures for my photography class.

Down at the bottom of the hill was a park with rainbows shining on the cement walls. Hundreds of little lights shone, creating beautiful chatoyant swashes, like thin fabric veils or oil in a puddle. Grant had a special pair of light-refracting glasses, and the tiny iridescent bulbs became prisms of their own radiance, each emanating jagged auroras of surplus light.

I didn't get to sleep until at least four thirty in the morning, but when I woke up at ten, I wasn't tired at all. We walked about six miles last night, but my energy was endless. I was in constant motion, bobbing around, dancing to the beats I heard in my head. My friends thought I was crazy, but I thought they were crazy too. We were all crazy last night. We were all the kings of our own worlds.

Infinite possibilities. Who knows what there could be in Arae? Only you will find out. Will you colonize there? Will you map it? As we stared up into space I mentioned to my friends that you were up there too, in your capsule. They didn't believe me. They said, "You're tripping."

What if the planet is already inhabited? In an infinite universe, how arrogant are we to assume that we are the only intelligent life form? What if while you're up there, aliens come and land on Earth? What then?

Discover new worlds, Mom. If it's what you want to do, then that is your prerogative. Compared to any of us on this planet, the many generations that will come and go while you're still traveling, still frozen in stasis, you, Mom, are infinite. You are eternal, you are timeless and we are mortal, our lives are very finite, we are already dead, I am already dead.

Your son,
William

May 25th

Dear Mom,

Dad met someone else. All those years of chastity, and for what? Faithful to a wife who he knew would never return, who never really was his wife to begin with, who had always been espoused to her dreams, her vision of space. For a wife and a mother aloof, always more interested in the stars than in him or me.

Dad's new girlfriend is Sophia. He started going to bars around the time when he realized that I

didn't want to hang out with him anymore, which he didn't realize until a few years after the fact. At one of them he met this woman. She's an architect on the design team for the new hospital. She also designed the courthouse. Speaking of which, those kids who blew up the courtroom all ended up getting caught. It was about six months later when the police burst through their door and arrested them all. They were totally unprepared; they thought that enough time had passed that the authorities wouldn't be looking for them, but bombing a court of law is no small deal. Now all five of them are in detention awaiting trial.

A month ago I got suspended for fighting. It was a fight that I started, and it was the first fight I'd ever been in. I boxed with my friend once, but that wasn't a fight, because we had both agreed to it beforehand, and we weren't angry at each other. That was just for fun. This wasn't. In my debate class, we had been discussing the merits of the space program. My argument was that though we gained new knowledge and would be able to carry our civilization on to the next frontier through exploration, the space program was detrimental to the family unit. I cited your absence as my example. The teacher liked my argument, and the guy I was debating wasn't able to rebut that aspect. Then this other person in the class, Fred, started mouthing off to me. He was saying, "Will, your mom's not in space, your mom's a whore. I saw her on Aurora, she was giving blowjobs for three bucks." I told him he'd better stop talking like that—so did the teacher and most of the other people in the class. He said, "My bad," acknowledging that he had done something wrong, but failing to actually apologize. I went and sat back down in my seat, but his seat's right behind mine, and he kept whispering things about you. Completely uncalled for, this hostility. Totally unprovoked. I was so frustrated, I felt like I had a fever, and I almost started crying.

At lunch, still fuming, I saw him outside with his friends who think they're cooler than everyone else. I walked over to him, and before he even noticed me, I slugged him as hard as I could in the jaw. "Fuck you, you faggot!" he yelled and started throwing punches at me. His friends formed a circle to barricade me in. They made catcalls and jeered as I tried to scrap with him, but he's bigger and stronger than me, and he's been in lots more fights. While he was coming at me, I was asking myself what the hell I had been thinking to come and start a fight with him. He socked me in the face, but I didn't go down, and I managed to get in a blow to his stomach, which knocked the wind out of him. We both backed off to momentarily recuperate. A crowd had gathered to watch. Some lunchtime entertainment for all the bored students, two humans brawling, duking it out for reasons apparent to none other than the combatants. He punched me one last time in the nose before an administrator showed up to break apart the fight. The crowd scattered, lest any of them be charged with incitation for their proximity to the duel. We were both sent home, with orders not to return for two weeks. Before I went over and punched Fred, I had handed my glasses to this girl I knew, who was eating lunch outside by herself. Two days into my suspension, she brought my glasses back to me at home.

Last week I went on a date with a girl, the same one who returned my glasses. She sat next to me in physics for a term this year. We would always have these nice little conversations, but we could never really talk all that much because the teacher would always tell us to shut up. All through my suspension, she and I texted back and forth. It took me awhile to work up the courage to ask her out, but the day I returned, I asked. Her face is soft, her features kind and gentle. She's so pretty I was intimidated, I was afraid that someone as pretty as her wouldn't want to date a guy like me. Then I started thinking that I really didn't care if she said no, because if she said no, at least I would have asked. At least I wouldn't have just let the moment pass by doing nothing. So I asked and she said yes. I took her out to get phở and we ended up staying in the restaurant for two hours, just talking. She asked me about you, and I told her how you were in space and how I would never see you again. Once I started talking about you it was hard for me to stop, but when I finally did I looked down and realized that she had put her hand over mine. She was looking at me with such solemnity that I knew she was someone I could trust, who I could really say anything to. Then she told me how her older brother had been killed three years ago in an attack on a subway. She speaks softly, but what she says carries weight. Her name is Valerie. I'm seeing her again tonight.

There was a report two weeks ago that NASA lost all contact with one of the shuttles. Speculation is that there was an error in charting the course, and the ship slipped into a black hole. Past its event horizon, nothing can escape, not even light. If even light cannot escape, black holes must have greater gravity than light has velocity. How could something be so powerful? But then, space itself, that black expanse, was powerful enough to suck you away from us. Most of the missions have been recalled. The president got on TV and started shouting about how we'll never beat the Chinese if we let a setback like losing a ship full of astronauts stop us from continuing our space program, but the director of NASA said he didn't want to risk the chance that there could be other such errors. The mission to Arae was not mentioned as one being recalled though. Apparently there is no doubt that the course to Arae is faultless.

I can no longer try to anchor you. I will not be your ground control anymore. My voice is no more recognizable to you than an unknown flight director's. You are not eternal, you are just frozen. You may outlast me but you will not outlive me. Because right now, I am alive and you are dead. For as long as I live, you will be dead. And after I have departed,

you still will be no better off until you are eventually
born anew, but that won't be for hundreds of years,
and you will never have truly lived, for the entire
time you were meant to be alive, you were in stasis.
Unsatisfied with the life you had, you ended it to try
your luck with a new one. Remember how I said I
would fill your capsule? I have nothing more to fill
it with.

Your son,
William

# Averting Dawn
## *Jordan Skyler (Age 17)*

The sheets are twisted, and I am entangled. The air is rich with the aroma of temples in India, but the scent of skin lingers and the burning tobacco begins to overtake everything.

Abandoned clothes are strewn across the floor, the chairs, the desk, the bookshelf, from an earlier fit of passion. A few moments from now there will be a scramble of legs and arms in the cold to collect them, but I'm not worried about that. I'm only worried about one thing right now.

Safe.

My dark hair is a ruffled mess, and her red hair seems to capture her pillow under it. My torso is exposed, but the warm air hugs me as I gaze at her. We are such opposites. She's laid out on her back, and I'm pensively resting on my stomach; she's surely dreaming something sweet, because her pale lips have curled into an innocent smile—while I am wide awake and smoking beside her cracked window attempting to get the taste of her out. Yet we tangle together, body and mind, in a beautiful melody of rapid breathing and wandering fingertips.

Inhale, tugging smoke out of this fresh cigarette and bringing a sense of peace into my needy lungs; I'll hold on to this moment for as long as I can. Inevitably the smoke will find a way to escape, but it's there now. I'm cherishing it while I can.

Safe. I promised.

The light is pale but illuminates the room regardless. The roughed-up room is neat and put together on the nights I'm not in her life. The walls are a warm white, like the pillow beneath my elbows, the blanket she's snuggled into that rests on the small of my back, and the sheets wrinkled, sweaty, and almost lost in the chaos. A lone candle coupled with the glowing embers of incense and this precious cigarette protects from the dark. In the daylight this place seems like a hospital room, so clean, so crisp, but in the feel of night it transforms into a chaotic heaven.

Safe. I've promised to keep her safe.

Her breath escapes with little noises and gentle movements. Mine is exhaled into wispy gray clouds. A record spins in the distance, something classic, something soft.

Ashes fall gracefully into their place in a small glass dish. The sky outside the open window begins to lighten tenderly. I take another drag while the dread of the rising sun dawns on me. My gaze falls on her charming face and a smile slips onto my lips,

but quickly disappears with a sigh and the sting of guilt.

I extinguish the embers that fight to glow at the end of my cigarette, lace my fingers, and shut my eyes. A headache is eagerly approaching, as is the day. I wish to push back morning and just stay in this moment. I'd light another cigarette and draw out the time, but it wouldn't help the situation. Sometimes I think we can't be helped, and most the time—I'm perfectly fine with that.

Safe, I've promised to keep her, though I can't seem to protect her from me.

# The Brick House
*Rose Owen (Age 15)*

Rain runs down the brilliantly clean windows, spattering the lawn and muddying the garden. It glitters in the air like tiny diamonds, refracting the colors through tiny facets. In front of a house, the arms of a tree, covered in mossy brown bark, lift and open to greet the water. Bruised purple plums pull at them, heavy and ripe and ready to be plucked. Brilliantly green leaves sprout from the branches like bursts of bright color against the cloudy, gray sky.

Though the tree is big, it is nothing compared to the house behind it. The house itself is not so tall, but its majestic character gives it the illusion of a towering skyscraper. The door is a dark, polished oak with a shiny handle carved in the shape of a roaring lion. Ivy curls up the brick walls, crumbling the mortar and pale orange blocks, tickling the expansive shell of the house. There is a merry homeliness about the place that lights up and warms the air around it. It is not only a house, but a home, glowing with years of hugs and jokes and family dinners. There's a love that makes you smile as you pass it. A love that turns the vacant windows cheerful.

From inside, however, you can see the truth. The rooms are empty and cold, with no furniture to fill them and no heat to warm them. The windows are blank slates that light the house with the pale, unearthly gray that radiates from the clouds outside. Dust blankets the floor, huddling in nooks and crannies, adding to the colorless, cold nature of the place. Memories of the happiness that this house used to hold echo through the empty spaces. In the corner of one room, there is a girl. Though she huddles there, it is no longer her home. She hides from the memories these walls hold, flinching from them even as they are called up in her mind.

The cold has slowly seeped into her, making her shiver, her teeth chatter. Two threadbare blankets attempt to keep her warm, but it's no use. The cold is not only in the air, it's in her blood, in her heart, in her very bones. The walls emanate it; the floors are frozen from it. She's not in the cold, she is the cold.

She might have been pretty once with sleek, dark hair, ivory skin, and deep blue eyes, but now her skin is a blotchy pink. Her eyes are swollen and red-rimmed with dark navy bruises beneath them. Her hair is slicked to her scalp with grease, and it frizzes eccentrically at the ends. Her lips are bitten and chapped, scabby and scraped. Tears run silently down her cheeks, salty sweet and bitter.

She rocks back and forth, back and forth, back and forth.

It didn't used to be this way. The outside appearance of the house is not a total lie. The girl can remember when it was warm here. She can remember when the rooms were not bare. She can remember when the light was soft and yellow and there was a family that was whole and loved each other. She can remember everything.

*Three Months Ago*

Firelight danced merrily across the walls, flickering across the faces of those gathered around it. A mother, bright eyed and smiling as she watched her children. A father, his arms wrapping comfortably around his wife. A daughter, barely fifteen, bouncing a giggling child on her knee. A son, the giggling child, barely a toddler, incoherent with giddiness after experiencing his first snowfall.

"Sled. Snow. White," Thom babbled, his round cheeks rosy, his bright sky blue eyes so like his sister's. The words stuttered excitedly off his young tongue, new and barely used.

The mother, father, and daughter chuckled at his childish innocence.

"That's right, little guy. That was snoooow." Sara drew out the word and reached around her brother's back to tickle him. Her dark hair was damp from sledding, and her blue eyes were slightly glazed, but adrenaline still rushed through her blood, lighting her veins with warm, wiry energy.

The mother and father gazed at them proudly, remembering their first snowfall and sighing with relief that their teenage years were over.

"Sara, honey, why don't you put Thom to bed? He's probably exhausted, and it's very late for him to be up anyway," Margaret, the mother, said in her kind, soft voice. The voice of a parent. Who knew it would ever turn so sharp as to cut her daughter?

"Yeah, okay," Sara agreed and left. Thom babbled on happily, sitting on her hip, only half of his words articulate enough to be understandable. Sara smiled and nodded as though she understood all of it. Thom's voice faded steadily as they walked upstairs.

Margaret turned to her husband. The fire had warmed him, the happiness of his children softening him.

"We should tell Sara, soon," she said. "It's only going to upset her more the longer we wait, and we have to start packing soon. It's not fair to her. This is her home just as much as it is ours. She should know." Her voice was hesitant, but firm, as she said it. She didn't want to believe what she was saying, but she had to. She knew it was true.

Alan, her husband, rubbed his forehead, closing his eyes. His wife's words slammed him back to reality with the harshness of clear, freezing water on warm, sleepy skin. The happiness of the recent family moment was swiftly disappearing, dread creeping in to replace it. "I know, Margaret. But I don't see you any more eager to do it than I am. She's going to hate us, and you know how she can get when she's angry..."

*Her words slammed him back to reality with the harshness of clear, freezing water on warm, sleepy skin.*

"She's a teenager, Alan. She's going to hate us sooner or later, no matter what we do, and we're going to have to deal with the consequences. She's going to be even angrier at us if we don't tell her before the movers come."

Alan sighed. Weariness, the weight of growing old that seemed to press down on him more and more those days, laced the sound.

"You're right. But we should wait one more day. She's so happy and tired, we can't throw this at her now," he said, partially believing it, and partially just wanting to put off what had to be done. Just one more day…

"Fine, but that's it. Tomorrow, we tell her." Margaret pecked Alan on the cheek decisively. Her mind was made up. Alan knew better than to argue.

*Present*

The worst part, the part that tears up Sara's insides, bleeding her till she is raw and empty, is that she knows she deserves this. She hadn't meant to do it. Hadn't wanted to. But she had.

It was her fault. All her fault.

Back, forth, back, forth she rocks. She can't stop, can't falter. The tears still run, though she feels so empty that she cannot figure out where they came from anymore. She feels dry, sapped of everything that makes her human, everything that matters. Left here with the dust and the blankets and the guilt.

The guilt. That's what's left. All that's left. It hangs everywhere, like sickly sweet honey in the air, filling her lungs as she gasps for breath. She's drowning in it. Drowning on dry land. Drowning in a room full of nothing.

Back, forth. Back, forth. Back, forth.

She has been tossed aside. No one wanted to deal with her, so they left her for the next people who lived here to deal with. She is now someone else's problem.

It started so early, she cannot even remember the beginning. Though her memory is better than most, who could reach into the darkness of the first months of life and pluck out coherence? There is something, though. She isn't sure if it is reality or fiction, but it is a memory and she clings to it.

*Twelve Years Ago*

Sara walked down the stairs. They were so big compared to her that she had to bend her knee completely every time she took a step. Her hands grasped at the rail for dear life, most of her weight placed there instead. She stumbled and tripped as many times as she took a successful step, but she made it to the bottom of the stairs. A smile lit her face. Her eyes glowed, her cheeks dimpled. She tiptoed toward the doorway. Her parents didn't react too kindly when she got up after bedtime, but she was so very thirsty. It couldn't hurt to just get a glass of water.

Voices bounced off the walls toward her. Deep, big people voices. She smiled again to hear those voices of the people she adored. Bright, shiny people. Her parents.

"There's something not right. You know that. And it's getting worse," her father said to her mother. His voice was agitated. It made Sara's heart sink to hear that tone.

*I didn't want a child yet. I told her we weren't ready.*

Sara stumbled back as the thoughts washed over her, faster and bigger than the voices. Tidal waves that hit her with a slamming force. The thoughts surrounded her, crushed her. Her tiny feet didn't make more than a swish against the floor. She tip-toed to the doorway, trying to hear more. Curious about something that could make her father's thoughts sound so big and angry.

"She is our little girl, and we love her." Her mother's tone was steely. Cold and metallic. A voice not asking for an argument, but braced for one. So different from the soft, kind voice Sara heard every day.

*Besides, what can we do?*

"There has to be someone we can talk to, someone who can help. We cannot deal with something like this on our own, Margaret. It's not normal." His voice lowered to barely above a whisper. It was hard on top, but cracked and smashed just beneath, like lasagna that's been left out on the kitchen counter for too long.

*It didn't say anything about this in the books.*

"And say what? That our daughter knows things she shouldn't? That she hears things people don't say? That sometimes things around her move when no one's touched them? Do you realize how insane that just sounded? And we know it's true!" her mother said. Young Sara flinched at her tone. That tone usually meant she did something wrong. That and pursed lips. Sara always got a time-out when her mommy's lips pruned up. She trembled at the thought of it now. What did she do wrong? She didn't know. She flattened herself against the wall. Hiding from the big people. They were having grown-up time. She didn't quite know what the things they were saying meant, but her mommy had prune lips for sure.

"I didn't sign up for this, Margaret. I could barely handle the idea of raising a normal kid, let alone a…a freak." His voice stumbled at the word, hesitating before he said it. His wife jerked back as though she'd been slapped. Her soft voice was even steelier than before. Her pursed lips tightened.

"I don't ever want to hear you call our daughter that again. Do you understand? You may not love her the way a father should, but I love her and I will not have you saying things like that in this house."

Her whole body tensed, her mouth rigid, eyebrows pulled down in an angry frown. She sat stick straight, her chin jutting forward in stubborn anger.

*If he loved her half as much as I do, he'd see why we can't tell anyone.*

Were they saying Daddy didn't love her? She couldn't tell. They were talking so fast. Their thoughts were angry and overwhelming, making her lean against the wall for support, her skinny legs too weak to hold her up. They reminded her of when she stepped on a little hill and wasps swarmed up and she got stung all over. Her mommy had gotten prune lips then too. But not angry-at-Sara prune lips, they had been angry-at-wasps prune lips.

In a different way, in the less decisive, more abstract way than a child could, in the way that Sara had understood that her mom's prune lips were at the wasps, Sara could understand what her parents were discussing. Could understand, but could not comprehend. A child who's been sunk too deep in the real world is still a child. She crawled back upstairs without her drink. She couldn't muster the strength to walk.

*Present*

Her fingernails are turning blue from the cold. She can see it. She's watched them get darker for a few hours. Deep, dark, ocean blue. She knows they should hurt. If it were any other time, they would. If this were any other time, she'd get up and turn on the thermostat. Now the thermostat doesn't work, disabled with no one to pay for it till the new people come. So she just stares at her nails, her eyes registering what her brain can't process. A computer given one too many orders, frozen in place. Heart still beating, metal still hot, but still and dead inside.

The tears have finally stopped running. Her skin tightens where the saltwater dries. Her eyes sting when she closes them. Dry sobs still make her shake and quiver and hack. Violent shivers break out like tiny, blood-boiling, bone-cracking, heart-jolting earthquakes.

The blankets flutter around her like worried grandmothers, not sure what they can do but anxious to help. They settle and resettle to cover every inch they can. Without even the flick of Sara's wrist, they move. She huddles and shivers, and they cover her like they care. Like it's not her mind causing it. Like they're actually worried.

Shake. Hack. Quiver. Wheeze.

Back. Forth. Back. Forth. Back. Forth.

She curls up on the floor, letting the blankets cover her. She wants darkness and quiet and peace. She wants to sleep.

She wants to die.

The blankets stop twitching and fall still over her at the thought.

Her nails are still blue.

*Two Months Ago*

Sara wasn't quite sure how it happened. First Thom was there, grinning at her, running his toy racecar over the hard counter he was perched on.

*Vroom, vroom.*

His thoughts made her giggle and he giggled too, seeing her smile.

Then he was on the ground. Fallen. *Thud. Crack.* Silence.

He was still. Still like no toddler would ever be. Limp, unnaturally still.

No, that wasn't right.

She'd been picking him up. He was heavy and soft and smelled like baby and peaches. He pushed at her, wanting to stay on the counter. Pushed and cried. Big toddler tears. Red cheeks and piercing wails.

She tried to hold on, tried to keep him in her arms. Pulled him closer, held him tighter. But he pushed and screamed, and she loosened her grip. Just for a moment, she didn't hold on quite so tightly.

Then he was on the ground. Fallen. *Thud. Crack.*

Silence.

Still.

But that wasn't how it happened either. She knew it even as it played in her head.

He'd been on the counter. The counter in the corner, so far away. Balanced precariously on the edge. She was worried. The kitchen floor was hard and tiled and unforgiving. She wanted him over by her, where she could catch him.

She went over, her feet slapping against the unforgiving floor. She wanted to bring him over where she could watch him, keep him from falling. She wanted to help.

She went over to get him.

She picked him up. She did. She felt him in her arms. Heavy and soft. Babies and peaches. Push. Fallen. *Thud. Crack.*

Silence.

Still.

Had she gone over?

She'd wanted him near her, where she could look after him. Save him from the tile. Keep the baby close. But she was baking chocolate chip cookies, the only thing she could bake. Her favorite dessert. Just out of the oven, fresh, moist, melted cookies. She was so close to finishing. Batter being stirred. *Whir. Whir.* She wanted to finish up. And wanted to get him, keep him safe. It was one of those little decisions that took her too long to make. She couldn't decide. Torn.

He moved. No, he didn't move. Well, he did, but she moved him. Except she was still all the way across the room. Pouring in the chocolate chips. The rich, velvety smell of chocolate floated into the air. She breathed in and looked over.

He was floating. Floating over the tile toward her. So she could keep him safe. Save him from the tile. That's all she wanted to do.

She saw him. He wasn't scared. He looked at the floor and looked at her and waved his arms. His little, stubby arms, waving, fingers outstretched. He smiled and laughed, earnest and childish in his excitement of being above the ground with nothing to hold him. He made his car zoom over the empty air.

But she'd seen him—stepped back and let go. Surprised. It was her doing it. Just moving him over. But she was startled. There was a little intake of breath. *Whoosh.*

Then he was tumbling down, fallen. *Thud. Crack.* Silence.

217

Still.

*Whir. Whir.*

Velvety chocolate. Baby and peaches.

Soft and warm and still.

"What did you do? What did you do?" Mom, Margaret, soft voice icy with dread. Shaking her.

Dad. Dad crying. Dad crying and picking up his son.

Dad crying and picking up his dead son.

*Present*

Sara gasps for air and opens her eyes.

No. It hadn't happened like that. He'd fallen. Fallen from the counter. Fallen on his own. It wasn't her fault. It couldn't have been her fault.

She sits up, leaning against the wall, knees to her chest. Rocking. Back, forth. Back, forth.

*Not my fault. Not my fault.*

She couldn't have done it. She was making cookies. She was all the way over on the other side of the room. She couldn't have done it.

Except she did. She moved him, without touching him, the way she so easily had with so many other things for so many years. All those other things had been so easy, felt so right. She'd thought it was boring, normal.

Then there was Thom. He wasn't a thing, he was a boy. Bouncing and giggling. It was too hard, too much to carry something so big and wild. She wasn't ready.

But she tried and she turned and there he was and she couldn't move him back and couldn't move him forward. He hung there, for just a second longer. Looking down, looking back up at her. Giggling and bouncing and waving.

*Vroom, vroom.*

Then he was falling.

And it was all her fault. She did it.

*Two Days Ago*

Sara's mom was in one of her rages. Her mom, who, up until Thom had di—, left, was the sweetest, softest mom she could ever hope for. The mom every other mother wished she could be. Now she was raging and screaming and crying. She didn't talk to the neighbors or play Scrabble with her husband or watch *Grey's Anatomy* with her daughter. They had take-out almost every night, and when they didn't, dinner was blackened or overcooked.

They'd retiled the kitchen.

"She is evil, the work of the devil, deranged. I will not have her in my new house." Her mother's scream drifted up the stairs into Sara's room, where Sara huddled in a corner, hiding from the fight. The blankets she sat on and a few dolls lined up in the corner were the only things they hadn't brought to the new house.

"Margaret, be reasonable. She's fifteen. Where is she going to go? You can't just decide you don't want her and throw her away. She's not some thing, she's your child." Her dad sounded weary, as he always did in those days. As if he just wished that everyone would be quiet so he could lie down and die already. Sara was too far away to hear their thoughts, but this was one of the times that she was glad about that.

"She is not my child. Thom was my child. She killed him. Murdered him. I couldn't give birth to a murderer. I couldn't raise a murderer, could I, Alan? Could I?" Her words were howls now, the sound raw and feral. Sara flinched from them. Tears ran down Margaret's face, uncontrollable sobs echoing from her throat.

"She is not a murderer. She did not kill Thom."

Even Sara could tell that he did not believe his own words. Doubt trickled through them, pulling and tugging at her father's conscience. Chipping away at his faith until it was peeled and torn, like worn-out paint, leaving nothing but the bare walls.

Her mom let out a sound somewhere between a hearty guffaw and a strangled wail.

"Even you aren't thick enough to believe that. Even you know that she is guilty. Weren't you the one who always said she wasn't natural, wasn't normal? Weren't you the one who called her a freak?"

"I was wrong to say those things." There was so much weariness. So much doubt.

"No, you weren't. You were right all along. She isn't our child. She's evil, and I will not keep her. Either she goes, or you both go, but either way she's not coming with me."

There was a pause, long and pregnant. Full of thoughts that were silent to Sara, as they would

be with any normal person. She couldn't hear the decision being made in her father's mind, but she knew what it would be.

"Fine."

And the door slammed as they walked out. The car rumbled. Gravel crunched. The rumbling faded.

*Present*

Violet plums pull at the arms of a tree outside. A tree that now droops with the weight of too much rain, sodden, sagging, and held down. The leaves glow green, healthy and full of life. Behind the tree is a brick house, ivy crawling up its walls. The rain pounds, cleansing and watering. It washes away the character of the house, the homeliness of it, like a mask of too much makeup worn by a desperate woman. Mascara runs, to reveal loneliness. Blush fades, leaving pallor. Lips lose color, and there is only sadness, emptiness, despair.

Inside, dust has taken over, making this place its new home. It blurs the sharp edges of the world, blending them like the watercolor of a child. There is no furniture and no heat, and it is freezing. In one room, in one corner, hides a girl.

A lost girl. A sad girl. A girl who has only just learned of the real world, where everything is not shielded from her by her mother's loving arms. A girl whose family was whole, but now is torn beyond repair. A girl who can remember everything.

# Contributor Q & A

Ink-Filled Page's contributors come from all over the United States, and some overseas too. We love getting to know them, and here, we share a few of their insights on the creative process with you.

### *Why do you write/create art?*

I create because I don't know any other way to breathe.
—Jacinda Williams, artist of "All Tied Up"

To get these toxins out of me, before they devour me.
—Jordan Skyler, author of "Averting Dawn"

### *What craft element do you find most challenging or intriguing (setting, character development, dialog, etc.)?*

It really varies from piece to piece. Ultimately, though, it's sometimes hard to find a subtle yet convincing way to convey your overall message without boring or insulting the audience.
—Christine Stoddard, artist of "Las Vegas"

I find artistic consistency and inspiration to be the most challenging element of my creative process.
—Ashley Kimbro, artist of "Juicy Cloud of Paradise"

For me, the criticism I get most often has to do with my endings or the denouement. Once my story has peaked, I often find myself stopping there. I like the idea that I am offering my reader a story with an infinite number of possible endings, but as my mentors and fellow writers have pointed out, doing this denies my reader the satisfaction of a story that is tightly woven from beginning to end. I'm not a big fan of tidy endings, so when I see another writer who can create an ending that is complicated yet satisfying, I am acutely aware of my own shortcomings.
—G. M. Hanson, author of "Powder Down"

*Do you ever find it difficult to create from a perspective that is not your own? How do you overcome this challenge?*

I love to stand on my head and look at the world from a different perspective. Working with children always helps this. Working with people always helps this.
—Jordan Skyler, author of "Averting Dawn"

I definitely have a much harder time creating something when it's someone else's idea. I feel the only way I can get over that is if I find a way to make it my own, even if I have to be sneaky about it.
—Jacinda Williams, artist of "All Tied Up"

*Discuss characters, places, or events that you find yourself returning to in your writing/art more than once.*

Everyone, including myself, is fair game. Be warned.
—Cecilie Scott, author of "I've Been to Jero Tapakan"

I write an inordinate amount about teenage girls. I think it's simply because I find them easiest to illustrate and relate to.
—Rose Owen, author of "The Brick House"

My common themes are angels, alcoholics, Portland, and relationship trouble. Oddly enough, my work is not autobiographical.
—Claire Rudy Foster, author of "Blue House"

## *Where is your favorite place to write/create?*

In my bedroom, with my cat sitting on the bed watching me.
—Jess Barnett, artist of "(I Promise) This Is the Last Time" and "Practice"

I have a big and sunny studio where I love to paint, a computer room for my writing and Internet adventures, a living room overlooking a ravine, and an orchard where I like to read and write journals and poems. I do feel fortunate to have all this space especially when the mornings are bright and the weather pleasant.
—Lea Goldman, artist of "Raven," "Political Argument," and "Meateater's Dilemma"

Any cafe that serves cinnamon buns will do.
—Aliya Whitely, author of "Strands"

## *How do you conquer the almighty blank page when writer's block (or the artist's equivalent) strikes?*

Clean canvases are delicious, and I love to start paintings. I have more ideas and beginnings than drive and patience to execute and complete them to my satisfaction. Many days I just wander around doing other things, and then it all comes naturally. It seems that the times when I do not create are incubation times. Then I think and dream about what I will do, and when the time is right, I do it.

—Lea Goldman, artist of "Raven," "Political Argument," and "Meateater's Dilemma"

Change media: use a pencil instead of a computer, or a typewriter, or somebody else's writing tools.

—Claire Rudy Foster, author of "Blue House"

What I do (and don't) recommend is just leave the piece alone until I find a new inspiration. Usually I only have to wait a few days. Writer's block is like forgetting a word that was on the tip of your tongue. All you have to do is stop thinking about the next event in the story, and it'll come back to you.

—Rose Owen, author of "The Brick House"

### When did you realize you were a writer/artist?

Well, actually, never. I still think I'm wandering around at doodler level but all my art teachers and friends have reprimanded me for lack of self-confidence so now I'm an artist. Yay?

—Annie Yang, artist of "Wishing Star"

I wrote my first "book" in third grade. It was the story of a monkey with superpowers who had to get to New York to intercept a shipment of magical bananas from falling into the hands of evildoers. It was a big hit with my teacher, and that's when I realized I loved creating stories. Everyone in my family is a terrific artist, but I can't draw at all. When I found that I could paint pictures with words, I started to feel like less of a black sheep. I still have a hard time self-identifying as a writer, especially when I read the skillful work of others. At this point in my life, I guess I see myself more as a storyteller who is trying really hard to become a writer.

—G. M. Hanson, author of "Powder Down"

A Wednesday morning in May 2001, around 5:30 a.m.
—Scott F. Parker, author of "On Shitting in the Woods and Other Tragedies of Running"

# Author Bios

## Sandra Arguello

Sandra Arguello is from Costa Rica. Currently, she is studying for a master's in publishing at PSU, where she also teaches Spanish. Though English is not her native language, she loves writing in her second language. In Costa Rica, she used to write for some newspapers and magazines like *The Tico Times* and *The Tourist*. For two years, she wrote a monthly column about life in her city, Heredia.

## Marian Burke

Marian Burke lives in Massachusetts with her children and is working on her second novel while she struggles to write the synopsis for her first.

## Caren Coté

Caren Coté grew up in rough neighborhoods in the San Francisco Bay Area. Between those streets and her cubicle in the Silicon Forest, she's passed through restaurants, bars, a newspaper with a staff of three, and a Hungarian flower shop. Her short fiction has appeared in *VoiceCatcher2* and on KBOO, Portland Public Radio.

## Alex Davis

Alex Davis, a graduate of Portland State University's Graduate English program, lives, hikes, and plays soccer in and around Portland. He works as an editor, freelance writer, and graphic designer on the side.

# Claire Rudy Foster

Claire R. Foster graduated with a BA in creative writing from Reed College. She lives in Portland, Oregon, with her husband and son. She is currently at work on her second novel.

# Andrew S. Fuller

Andrew S. Fuller grew up in Nebraska and other places, climbing trees and reading books. He lives in Portland, Oregon, where he spends his time writing stories and reading them. He is the sometime artist (or graphic designer or editor) of *Three-Lobed Burning Eye* magazine. He has published in *Abyss & Apex*, *Fantastic Metropolis*, *The Harrow*, *House of Pain*, *BloodRose*, and *A Fly in Amber*. He is the author of two poetry chapbooks and a graphic novella. He climbs rocks now. Learn more about him at *www.owlsoup.com*.

# Megan Guiney

Megan is a 2007 graduate of Stonehill College, where she studied English and the cinema. She is currently trying to figure out what she wants to be when she grows up.

# G. M. Hanson

G. M. Hanson is a recent graduate of UCLA and has just been accepted into California State University, San Bernardino's inaugural MFA program. Hanson lives with a menagerie of ill-behaved rescued animals and longs for the day when shed animal hair on black clothing becomes a chic fashion statement.

# Rose Owen

Rose, a freshman at Lincoln High School in Portland, Oregon, was exposed to literature at an early age by her mother. She was so taken with the written word that she never left home without a book in her hand. The love of writing simply stems from the larger love of the written word, and the feeling of creating something that someone else can read and experience is indescribably magical.

## Scott F. Parker

Scott F. Parker has a bad ankle right now. When it gets better he expects to run more and to start having trouble with his bowels again. He has written for several books in the Popular Culture and Philosophy series. "On Shitting in the Woods and Other Tragedies of Running" is part of his essay collection *The Joy of Running qua Running* (in progress).

## Danielle Rollins

Danielle Rollins is a professional freelance writer. Her work appears in *The Stranger*, *InterSections*, and *The Wig Fits All Heads*. Four of her short stories were finalists in the 2008 Long Story Short competition, and her first novel is under consideration for publication with a small press. She lives in Seattle, Washington, where she recently completed a BA in English. She is currently working on her second novel, a young adult book called *Imaginary*.

## Ian Sanquist

Ian is a senior at Garfield High School in Seattle, Washington, and enjoys the freedom of the literary medium, particularly how no one author is exactly like another. He is a writer for his school newspaper, *The Garfield Messenger*, and had a satire on bureaucracies published last year in *Perceptions*, the Mt. Hood Community College literary magazine. He will attend Western Washington University in the fall, where he plans to study journalism and literature.

# Cecilie Scott

Cecilie Scott left the Cascade foothills for Portland two years ago, trading pasture for garden and sheep for roses. She still works as a technical editor to pay for groceries, and writes to feed her soul. Current projects include a collection of linked stories about travelers in search of paradise and a travel memoir of Bali and cancer, *Knowing Bodies*. Her work has appeared in *Quality Fiction, Crab Orchard Review, The Healing Muse, The Dos Passos Review,* and *The Raven Chronicles*. She's maintained a Web site, *www.turtledreams.org,* for a dozen years.

# Jordan Skyler

Jordan, a junior at Lake Washington Technical Academy in Kirkland, Washington, is an artist of sorts; she writes, vandalizes, and captures lives with every unlaced step. She just wants to capture something, someone, anything, and everything. Writing and working through different experiences and storylines helps her understand them and how they shape people. She is currently working on several short stories by day and empty city walls by night—all while stumbling through technical school and awkward part-time jobs. J. D. Salinger and Stephen Chbosky are her inspiration.

# Malia Wagner

Malia Wagner was born and has so far been raised in Portland, Oregon, where she is a junior at St. Mary's Academy. She loves to write and was first inspired to write this story in eighth grade with the prompt "I Wonder." It has morphed a great deal since then. She thoroughly enjoys drinking Florida Orange blood.

# Aliya Whiteley

Aliya Whiteley lives in Buckinghamshire, England, with her husband and daughter. Her novel *Light Reading* was published by Pan Macmillan in April 2009.

# Artist Bios

## Jess Barnett

Jess Barnett is an abstract expressionist painter who lives and works in Boston. Her primary medium is acrylic, and her influences include Francis Bacon, Franz Kline, and Japanese calligraphy.

## Shannon Burckhard

For Shannon, a senior at Canby High School in Canby, Oregon, drawing is a great way to relax and be completely absorbed with the task at hand. She enjoys drawing in a realistic style, as she loves trying to replicate the details.

## Sarah Butcher

Sarah Butcher is an artist and teacher who lives and works in Baltimore County, Maryland. She has a BA in art from the College of Notre Dame of Maryland. Her artwork has been sold to interior designers and small galleries in the Baltimore area. Sarah teaches studio art, digital photography, and graphic design. Her recent artwork focuses on the overlooked and finds purpose for the discarded. Dried flowers, insects, and found objects provide an introspective analysis of the hidden beauty that exists in places not readily in view. Old paintings, magazines, and paint come together in collages that take a tongue-in-cheek look at modern culture. Sarah likes to think that she possesses a child-like curiosity that pushes her to pursue subjects that most people discard or never notice.

# Tina Christian

Tina Christian is a person best described as a blind enthusiast of all that is visual in art, stage, film, photography, laughter, and the outdoors.

# Elena Cronin

Elena Cronin's primary focus has always been figural work that portrays the organic qualities of the human body—perfection and flaw, awkwardness and grace, tension and fluidity. Her most recent work features first-person self-portraiture. She lives in Portland, Oregon. *www.elenacronin.com*

# Andrew Dean

Andrew Dean lives in Seattle where he is enjoying his last year of high school. He plans to explore photography beyond high school.

# Evan Geer

Evan Geer is a photographer who focuses on the experimental, abstract, and surreal. He aims to show the world as he sees it by using mixed media and digital manipulations, as well as old-fashioned 35mm film photography. He believes the world is far too complex for just one eye. Evan lives in Portland, Oregon.

# Lea Goldman

Lea Goldman is a full-time painter and printmaker. Her work is narrative in nature with close attention to abstract elements such as composition, texture, and form. Her interest in multicultural traditions, legends, and folklore has evolved into a personal mythology, constantly developing, and expressed in an array of art images and materials. Lea earned an MA in art from Columbia University in New York City and an MFA in studio arts from California State University, Los Angeles. Lea's prints and paintings have been exhibited in museums and galleries throughout the country, have received many awards, and were featured in numerous solo shows.

## Sarah Elizabeth Hicks

Lately, Sarah Elizabeth Hicks has been working on the art of self-portraiture through photography. It is a very interesting way to express herself as a photographer and as a woman. She uses her body as a tool to communicate her feelings and expressions, using the mood and tone to enhance the excitement and mystery behind the photograph. "When I look at my self-portraits, I really don't see them as me; I become merely a subject matter aiding this creative process." *www.sarahelizabethart.typepad.com*

## Ashley Kimbro

Ashley Kimbro is a poet, graphic designer, illustrator, and proverbial black sheep. In 2008, she graduated with honors, receiving a BFA from the Maryland Institute College of Art in Baltimore, Maryland. Ashley has since moved to a quaint home in Illinois where she writes, draws, and keeps a small window garden. She is relearning how to appreciate a good book and some peace and quiet. During occasional bits of spare time she can be found reading Austen or consuming mass quantities of tea (preferably Dragon Well). "Juicy Cloud of Paradise" was inspired by past preoccupations with heaven.

## Diane Leon

Diane Leon earned a BA in art history from NYU, an MA from the Draper Program, and a degree in humanities and social thought from the NYU Graduate School of Arts and Science. She believes that abstract painting gives her the freedom to create what she is feeling. Most of her work comes from decades of internalizing the Mediterranean coast of Spain.

# Gabby Raglione

Gabby is a junior at Lincoln High School in Portland, Oregon. In October 2008, Gabby traveled to Africa to bring AIDS relief and hope to the people of Mutare, Zimbabwe. The children there were some of the most beautiful things she had ever seen and had much to do with her inspiration.

# John Stack

John Stack was born in 1985. He began painting and drawing at a young age and continued making art throughout high school and college. John graduated from Alfred University in 2007 with a BFA, focusing on illustration, painting, and video. He has assisted a record label and a film and production company with multiple projects, and he recently assisted an art director on the set of an independent film. John works at a design company. You can view his artwork online at *www.johhny-stack.com*.

# Christine Stoddard

Christine Stoddard is writer, fashionista, and interdisciplinary artist from Arlington, Virginia. She currently lives in Richmond, Virginia, and studies creative writing at Virginia Commonwealth University. You can read her writing at *www.associatedcontent. com/christinestoddard* and view her art on the Facebook group Christine's Cognitive Chaos. You can also sample her music project at *www.myspace.com/christinestoddardblameslarks*.

# Kyle Tabuena-Frolli

Kyle, a senior at Independence High School in San Jose, California, finds that the quality of a picture depends on location, light, movement, and color. He is constantly inspired by the environment because, to him, almost any picture can be great with a stunning background.

## Jacinda Williams

An aspiring photographer, Jacinda Williams is trying to keep the tradition of actual film photography alive. She believes that there is nothing more beautiful than a truly real black-and-white photo.

## Annie Yang

Annie is a freshman at Lynbrook High School in San Jose, California. She was inspired one night while looking out her window into the night sky. She found it interesting how so many people could be connected through such a simple act, like looking at the stars, without ever really thinking about it.

## Boguslav Yanishen

Born in a musical family, Boguslav was surrounded by creativity, wanting to draw for as long as he can remember. He tried watercolors, tried color pencils, even tried oil paintings, but could never find satisfaction until one day in class, he started to draw with a red pen. He is currently a junior at Centennial High School in Portland, Oregon, and also attends CAL, the Center for Advanced Learning, where he is in a graphic design program. On top of school, he works at a design studio and plays bass guitar in a wedding band.

# Editor Bios

## Ali McCart
### *Senior Editor*

Ali thinks her love for the written word might have something
to do with the pungent odor of ink and the methodic sounds
from her parents' printing press, which permeated her senses
before she even knew how to read. She has a bachelor's degree
in English from Willamette University and a master's degree in
book publishing from Portland State University. She's written
and edited for periodicals in Oregon, Idaho, and Montana and
edited for authors and book publishers across the country. She
also spent two years as a bookseller and sometimes still itches to
create front-of-store displays. When she's not editing, reading, or
sneaking whiffs of local print shops, Ali spends her time hiking
with her dog, traveling, and feeding the geese at the park near
her house.

## Kim Greenberg
### *Production Editor*

Between memorizing fairy tales as a toddler and stalking the
local bookstore, it's been a given that Kim's life would revolve
around books. Leaving sunny California for the much greener
Portland, Kim recently finished up her senior year as an English
major, religious studies minor at Lewis & Clark College. She is
eagerly exploring the next stage in her life. She is lucky enough
to be the editorial intern at Indigo, learning all about the publishing industry and the literary world while reading through

submissions for *Ink-Filled Page* and tackling the Editorial Tip of the Week. Kim can usually be found on an armchair, a copy of Austen in one hand and a young adult novel in the other.

# Kori Hirano
## *Production Editor*

Growing up with a book in one hand and a pen in the other, Kori has deep love and appreciation for the written word. After earning a degree in English from the University of Oregon, Kori moved to Portland to get involved in the thriving arts community. In the past two years, she has done volunteer work for a theatre company and the nonprofit Write Around Portland, and is now learning about the editing process as an intern at Indigo. When Kori is not reading submissions for Indigo's quarterly online literary journal, *Ink-Filled Page*, she is creating spreadsheets at her day job, perusing the books at Powell's, or catching up on her movie list.

# Hannah Kingrey
## *Production Editor*

Hannah's recent literary adventures include: enduring a hot and dusty taxi ride through a sprawling Dakar suburb to learn about publishing in Senegal's indigenous languages; catching up on thirty years of women's writing at Calyx Press in Corvallis; and spending hours at the University of Oregon Special Collections library, poring over writer Molly Gloss's thoughts on wilderness, women who homesteaded, and Sasquatch. In addition to *Ink-Filled Page*, Hannah has enjoyed working on the Robert D. Clark Honors College publication, *Chapman Journal*, and *CALYX: A Journal of Art and Literature by Women*. Hannah might be spotted at her local library, loading up on feminist writing, sci-fi, gardening and cooking books, spiritual texts, graphic novels, as well as various and sundry stories about rural life, surreal fantasies, and other fabulous redheads.

# Megan Wellman
*Production Editor*

Megan's love for words began underneath the branches of her grandparent's oak tree, where she devoured book after book. A handful of years later, Megan earned her BA in English Literature from Western Washington University. After graduation she decided to turn her obsession with reading into a career and began working as an editorial assistant at Illumination Arts Publishing Company in Bellevue, Washington. Megan graduated from the publishing program at Portland State University last fall. Although her literary tastes have changed from *The Very Hungry Caterpillar* to *Jane Eyre*, Megan still visits the oak tree from time to time.

# Kelsey Connell
*Proofreader*

Kelsey Connell recently received her Bachelor of Arts degree in English with a business minor from the University of Oregon Clark Honors College. Seemingly born a bibliophile and writer, she was seldom far from books, pencil, and paper. This passion continued in her years at UO where she created and was editor-in-chief of *Unbound*, a student-run online literary magazine. She also spent a large part of her senior year delving into flash fiction with the Kidd Tutorial Intensive Writing program. She brings her love of short fiction and nurturing authorial creativity to the team at Indigo. She enjoys fro yo (frozen yogurt), music, and, most recently, biking on her turquoise cruiser.

# Lisa McMahan
*Proofreader*

Lisa McMahan is studying English and German Studies at the University of Portland, where she is a writer for the school newspaper. Growing up, she visited the La Grande Public Library every week and can still recall the musty smell of its basement. She routinely checked out the maximum amount of books permitted and resorted to carrying them home in a plastic milk crate with her sister. Lisa spent her sophomore year living in Salzburg, Austria, where she discovered her affinity for traveling, sauerkraut, and German beers.